D0781707

ARCHITECTURAL DELINEATION

Presentation Techniques and Projects

James T. Davis, MFA and James C. Watkins, MFA

Second Edition

KENDALL/HUNT PUBLISHING COMPANY
4050 Westmark Drive   Dubuque, Iowa 52002

Contents

Student drawings on this page by Tony Saenz and Jaime Montoya, isometric drawing on right by J. Davis.

Cover illustrations by David Farrell, AIA, Good Fulton and Farrell Architects : and student illustrations by Ryan Bemberg, Eric Tice and Jason Darling.

SHADE AND SHADOW STUDY

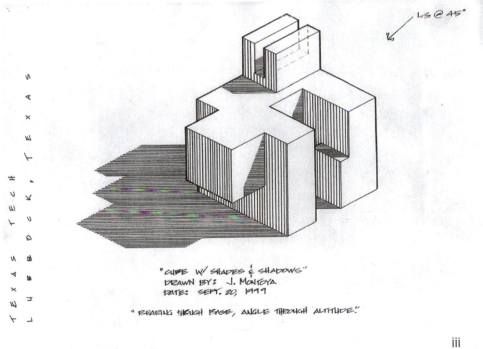

TEXAS TECH, LUBBOCK, TEXAS

Ls @ 45°

"CUBE W/ SHADES & SHADOWS"
DRAWN BY: J. MONTOYA
DATE: SEPT. 20, 1999

"BEARING THROUGH BASE, ANGLE THROUGH ALTITUDE."

Dedication

To my mother and grandmother who never let me say "can't" and kept me supplied with pencils and drawing paper.
JCW

To my wife, Evelyn Davis, for her infinite patience.
JTD

Acknowledgements

We wish to acknowledge the following people for their full support and input into this project.

Thanks to Wesley Phillips, our production manager. This project would never have been accomplished in a timely manner without his expertise and commitment.

Thanks to Dean James E. White of the Texas Tech College of Architecture for his support and encouragement.

Thanks to our readers: Evelyn Davis, Karen DeWitt and Sara Walters/Watkins—your advise genuinely is appreciated.

Thanks to our student assistants: Stacy Goolsby, Jason Moore, Jaime Montoya and Tony Saenz for their hours of unquestioned labor.

Thanks to instructors Julianne Jay and Micah Land for the contributions with exciting new projects.

We would like to express our utmost appreciation to our students and to the professionals in the field of architecture whose work appears in this publication. Your love for drawing is a constant inspiration.

Student pen and ink drawing by Brent Wright, field study in pencil by James Watkins.

FOREWORD…Virginia Mahaley Thompson

To state the obvious is not always a bad beginning. As children we loved to draw! We drew for pure delight and expression, we drew for communication and story telling, we drew for understanding and interpreting the world around us through the very act of drawing. Systematically, we learned new languages with their governing principles, possibilities and limitations. **We forgot to draw.** As with any language, constant use and practice are necessary to retain skills and attain higher degrees of accomplishment.

For architects drawing is a connection between past, present and future. Not only personal memories, but rich historical records of architecture are preserved through drawing. Thoughts emerging from conceptual sketches into more refined drawings and coming to full birth as "building" are witnessed throughout architectural history. Drawing allows the architect to see, and to show to others things which are to be…the prophecy of a future. Simply put, architects draw to make buildings. Architects draw to help sculpt the future.

Equally important reasons for the architect to draw are: drawing is art; architecture is art; drawing and architecture communicate concepts of civilization. Since the beginning of time humans have created drawings and architecture to express civilization and their feelings for it.

Drawing has been an integral part of the architectural program at Texas Tech since its beginning and has consistently earned the respect of the architectural community statewide. The architectural program at Texas Tech received its first accreditation from the National Architectural Accrediting Board in 1957. At that time, drawing was cited as a strength in the program; in successive accreditations since the first visiting team, drawing continues to be commended as an area of excellence in the architectural program. In early times, multiple freehand classes, life-drawing, watercolor, and sculpture were part of this segment of the architect's education. With changes in architecture, both professionally and academically, this area was gradually reduced and compacted into two courses. Mechanical drawing, which in earlier years was part of the design studio, was also integrated into the two-course sequence. This concentration of materials demands teachers committed to well-organized, streamlined syllabi. Professors Watkins and Davis have responded to this challenge. I know them to be committed to artistry in the architect's education. At this time it is more important than ever to have personal human interaction between teacher and student. Computers allow quick investigation of multiple design ideas and visualizations; however, an understanding of drawing concepts known only through direct eye-mind-hand creations sets up insights, which allow the student to use the advantages of computer drawings in meaningful ways. I have found that students who excel in freehand drawing adapt their talents very easily to the tools of computer graphics. Unfortunately, this does not seem to follow in the reverse order.

Sitting face to face with a client, spontaneously developing sketches which express both client's and architect's concepts is an exceptional talent and an invaluable design method. Original ideas will no doubt evolve as the architecture develops. The initial conceptual sketches are a great artifact linking back to a history, a thought process, and they are a beautiful thing in themselves.

Freehand drawing assures a direct personal involvement of the architect in the architectural act.

Virginia Mahaley Thompson
Associate Professor Emeritus

Preface

My co-author, Jimmy Davis and I are both artists who teach drawing to architecture students. As artists we approach drawing with the point of view that the phrase "to see" is of prime importance. As Teilhard De Chardin stated "the whole of life lies in the verb seeing." We want our students to become intense observers. This kind of acute observation opens up endless possibilities that lead to moments of clarity and inspiration.

To really see something, that is, to see all of its subtleties and not just to identify it, is a skill that can be learned gradually through the drawing process. The result is life enhancing.

On many occasions I've had students come to me after taking the delineation sequence, and state that their lives have been enriched and changed forever because of their experience in the drawing studio. These students demonstrate through their work a visual keenness and visual passion. They no longer take the world around them for granted, which is a main ingredient for becoming a critical thinker.

In these days of computer mania, the fact remains that freehand drawing is the ultimate tool for sensitizing a person to the colorful, shape filled world around us.

This book is the result of never being completely satisfied with the various instructional books that we've used over fifteen years of teaching architectural drawing. As a result we've used many different books simultaneously to balance deficits found in each. Our goal is to provide exercises that increase visual awareness, develop drawing skills and confidence in each serious student who uses this book. Each project is designed to give the student cumulative information while reviewing previously acquired skills. We feel that the discipline of seeing (by way of drawing) is an end in itself. It makes the individual more intimately aware of the external world and the internal world of ideas.

James C. Watkins

"... Only drawings can animate. They remain the most effective way of exploring the elusive questions of light and scale." I. M. Pei, FAIA

Introduction

The intent of this text is to provide an introduction to delineation techniques and to present an overview of application of basic drawing and painting for rendering. It includes instructional and motivational examples of both student and professional work. It is not designed as a definitive text on any single aspect of drawing or media and technique. Its purpose is to provide a series of experiences for students that will result in a foundation for continued aesthetic growth and development.

To a great extent the computer is usurping hand drawing as a general means of graphic communication in the minds of many educators today. In most design fields CAD (computer aided design) is the preferred way to produce working drawings. However, the inherent beauty and personal connection of the "human touch" are difficult to imitate through technology. Most people, employers and clients alike, still appreciate the skillful application of hand drawing and rendering. Freehand drawing builds a basic vocabulary for visual communication.

Introductory experiences such as quick sketching and contour line drawing establish a foundation for development of drawing skills. Observation of the environment through drawing contributes to heightened visual sensitivity. Specific exercises directed toward design drawing experiences prepare students for architectural design classes. The act of drawing always involves problem solving and application of principles of composition.

Watercolor is the medium traditionally associated with architectural presentation renderings. However, today the speed and convenience of certain technologies such as ink markers have resulted in a lessening of emphasis being placed on watercolor for many architectural students. In some schools, architecture students are not provided an opportunity to experience watercolor as a part of their curriculum. In the College of Architecture at Texas Tech University there is a long standing tradition of teaching basic watercolor techniques as a means of enhancing design drawings as well as for more formal presentations renderings. An exposure to and a degree of mastery in this medium provides a meaningful connection to tradition, an opportunity for general aesthetic development and a valuable tool for communication of graphic ideas. Additionally, watercolor is an effective vehicle for teaching color theory, composition and design principles.

We feel that exposure to freehand drawing and traditional media gives our students an edge over students in programs where all presentation work is limited to CAD applications. Freehand drawing in a variety of media, including watercolor, is still a necessary and valuable tool for the designer to supplement and complement mechanical drawing and CAD skills.

James T. Davis

Learning to Draw

Fluency in graphics communication is expected from architects and designers. These essential skills of visual communication are developmental and the process of assimilation takes time. The advent of CAD (computer aided design) caused some people to believe freehand drawing skills are unnecessary. The converse is true. The computer is certainly a powerful tool when added to the designer's tool chest, but it does not replace ones ability to visualize ideas with pencil and paper. Visual sensitivity and creativity develop during the intimate process of drawing.

The process of learning to draw involves development of eye, mind and hand coordination and simultaneously the development of visual sensitivity. Guided observation in a classroom setting assists the student in learning what to look for and how to selectively focus. For instance, students must make appropriate choices concerning what aspect of a subject to simplify, emphasize or diminish. The most common mistake by beginners is not having focus or focusing on irrelevant detail. Practice at drawing increases the eye, mind and hand coordination. In other words, to learn to draw one must draw. Of course there are certain rules of application and convention that must be learned for specific design areas such as multi-view drawing, paraline drawing, and constructed perspective drawing. However, beyond the rules the ability to draw evolves through the act of drawing.

The initial drawing exercises presented here are a series of activities, which promote visual sensitivity and develop basic skills needed for any graphic communication. Just as an athlete trains with exercises that may not appear to relate directly to his or her specific sport, a potential architect or designer benefits from directed visual experiences, which help develop visual sensitivity. Skipping rope does not look like boxing, lifting weights or attending ballet class does not resemble a football game, but these activities certainly contribute to important physical development for these sports. In a similar manner, drawing ones hand or shoe may not look like skills directly needed by architects or designers yet they contribute greatly to relevant visually growth. At first, the specific subject matter is not important. The activity of focused observation and problem solving is crucial.

black & white

Student drawings, cap by Jesus Robles, elevation/fenestration study by Sam Lin.

Using the Pencil as a Visual Tool

The pencil may be used as a tool to aid in determining angles, proportion and alignment.

To assist in measuring the proportion of objects, hold the pencil at arm's length. Close one eye. Measure from the point to your thumb. Bring the pencil down to your paper and draw the same measurement. Be sure to extend the arm at the same distance each time to insure a consistent measurement and alignment.

To assist in finding the correct angle and alignment, hold the pencil at arm's length. Close one eye. Align the pencil with the object. Bring the pencil down to your paper and draw the same line.

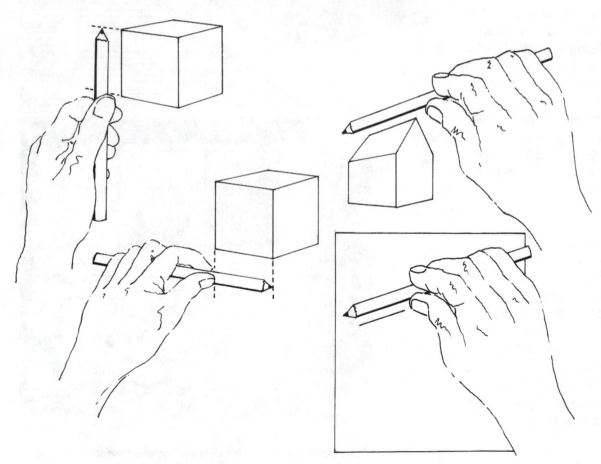

How to Hold a Pencil

By holding the pencil in a relaxed manner you are able to use the whole body and arm to draw. This position promotes loose and expressive drawing. Holding the pencil in a writing position is useful for detailed drawing which demand precision and control.

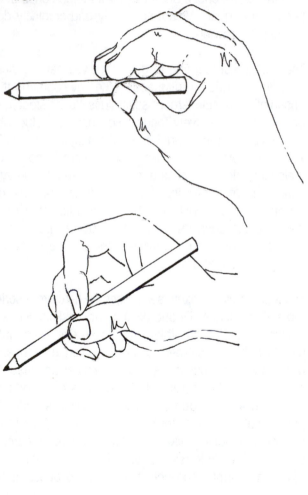

Quick Sketching for Visual Acuity

Drawing is the visual language of architects, artists and designers. Drawing is our most vital form of visual communication; it is essential in communicating ideas whether it be in the studio on the drawing table, on the back of a napkin or a piece of plasterboard. Quick sketch exercises may be given to increase skills and confidence in drawing. Learning to see with visual acuity can be gained through the physical act of drawing. Marked improvement may be achieved by daily five and fifteen minute quick sketch exercises.

Goals

This exercise teaches students how to express ideas quickly with clarity. The use of quick sketch exercises helps to improve hand-eye coordination and fine tune observational skills related to perspective, proportion and scale.

Methodology

Slides are used to project images of buildings, entourage, and landscapes. Five minutes sketches are used as warm up exercises. Fifteen minutes exercises are expected to communicate a complete idea. The pencil may be used as a tool to aid in determining angles, proportion, and alignment (as shown in the illustration).

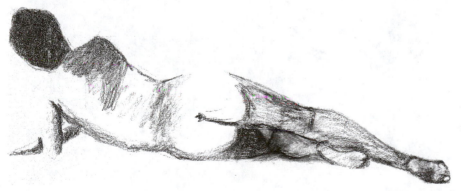

Student drawing by Brock Bejcek, graphite on 9" x 12" drawing paper. 10 minutes.

Student drawing by William Evan Figueroa, graphite on 18" x 24' drawing paper. 10 minutes

Student drawing by Ryan Meyer, graphite on 9″ x 12′ drawing paper. 15 minutes

Student drawing by Josh Barta, wash and ink on 9″ x 12″ drawing paper. 15 minutes.
Student drawing by Tyler Kruse, graphite on 9″ x 12″ drawing paper. 15 minutes.

4

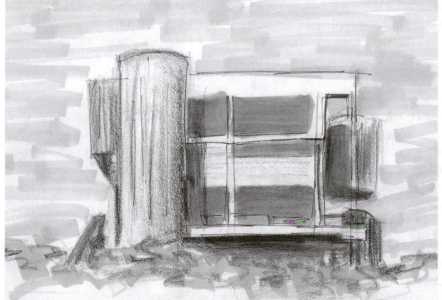

Student drawing by Ryan Meyer, graphite on 9″ x 12″ drawing paper. 5 minutes
Student drawing by Rebecca Weems, wash and graphite on 9″ x 12″ paper. 10 minutes

Student drawing by Ryan Meyer, graphite on 9″ x 12′ drawing paper. 15 minutes

Kimon Nicolaides said, "Learning to draw is really a matter of learning to see – to see correctly – and that means more than merely looking with the eye." The process of drawing teaches us to see, to analyze and to observe. Naturally, it is easier to draw things that we know. Therefore, many of these initial exercises explore process through observation of familiar subject matter.

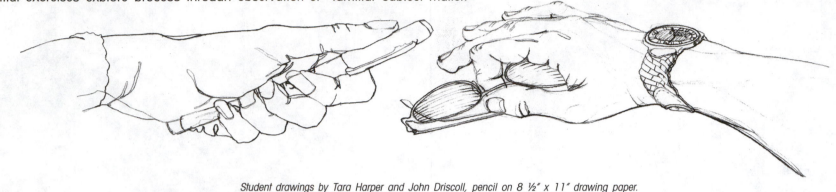

Student drawings by Tara Harper and John Driscoll, pencil on 8 ½" x 11" drawing paper.

Modified Contour Line Drawing

For artists, architects or designers, line is one of the most useful and potentially expressive elements at their disposal for visual communication. Line may delineate sharply defined edges of a three-dimensional form or the boundary of a flat shape, or it may simply indicate incisions on a surface. It may imply a general directional movement or it may blur the separation between parts. Lines may be even and regular, or modulated and varied in thickness or weight. They are used to establish an axis (a dominant direction). Lines communicate expression through their character. They may be nervous, dependable, fast, slow, rigid or sensuous. Lines can even suggest texture, mass, light and shadow. They describe form and create mood. All of these effects may be exploited deliberately or instinctively. When we draw, line is commonly used to establish or describe the contour of an object.

Goals

The objectives for this and subsequent projects are to enable the student to develop observational skills, to become aware of mass and skeletal structure inherent in the contour of form. Additionally, through the process of these exercises the student becomes more aware of proportion, composition (placement on the page or within a frame shape) and the development of line quality. Concepts to be emphasized with modified contour line drawing are controlled observation, contour lines that describe the surface of the form not just a silhouette, various applications of line quality, composition, proportion and skeletal structure.

Methodology

Instructions are: Use a soft pencil (Ebony) on sketch paper, draw your hand as a modified contour line drawing. Hold your hand away from the paper. Look at your hand, not the paper (90% of the time, you should occasionally glance at the paper for control and to acquire more accurate proportion.) Imagine you are touching the surface of your hand with the point of the pencil as you draw. Draw slowly and deliberately. Vary the pressure of the pencil as you move the line over the page. Try to avoid picking up the pencil as you draw, keep it in contact with the surface of the page. Draw as close to life size as possible, within an 8 ½" x 11" format.

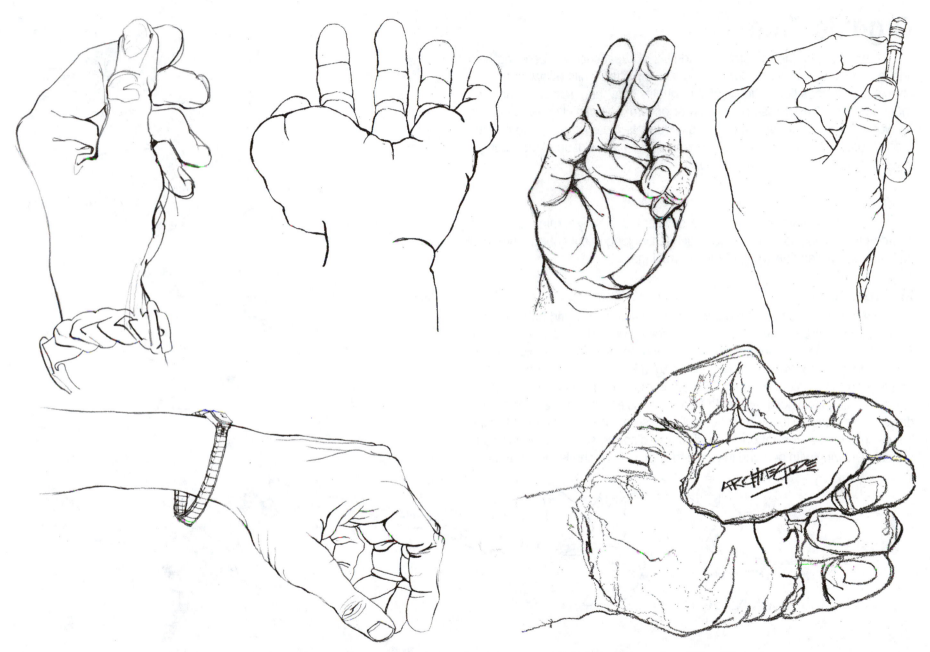

Student drawings by Brad Hackler, Amber Dawn Storer, Jose Maese, Chris Sturm, Tara Harper and Ruel Mendoza, pencil on 8½" x 11" drawing paper.

Organic Form

The drawing of plant forms provides additional experience in observing how line is used to describe contour and skeletal structure while allowing for emphasis on composition. Variety of line quality may be stressed without as much concern over precise proportion or accuracy of depiction of the object as was the case while drawing hands. Students are encouraged to employ greater "artistic license" in size relationships and visualization of the arrangement of form within the frame shape.

Goals

The basic goal of this exercise is the development of eye, mind and hand coordination. Students learn to make qualitative judgements about composition and use varied line weight in their drawings.

Methodology

Students are asked to collect plant forms as subject matter and bring them to class. Examples of similar drawings are shown prior to the drawing exercise. Each student places a plant on their desk and observes it for a few minutes before beginning to draw. They are encouraged to visualize the image of their drawing on the blank page before a mark is made on the white paper. They are told to simplify what they see, to search for the essence of the form as they draw. The procedure followed is basically the same as for the drawings of the hand. The media, format and time limit are also the same as the previous project. Drawing with pen and ink instead of pencil is a challenging variation.

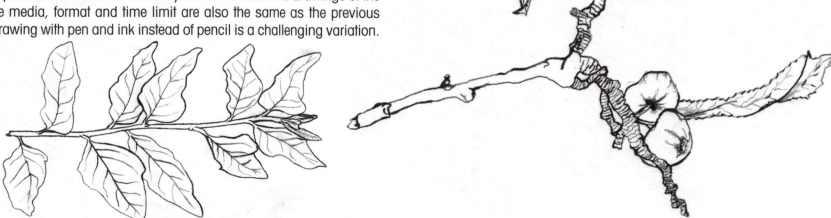

Student drawings by Keith Kelly, Daniel Pruske and Ty Summers, pencil on 8½" x 11" drawing paper.

Student drawings by Keith Leibfarth, Mark Carpenter, Ruel Mendoza, Scott Snyder, Tara Harper, and Daniel Pruske, pencil on 8½″ x 11 drawing paper.

9

Simple Still Life

The third exercise in this series is an outside of class assignment. The student composes an arrangement of small objects for drawing with a pencil.

Goals

This exercise is a test of retention of concepts previously presented. All three of these exercises (hand, organic form, and simple small objects still life) are good for developing basic drawing skills, especially learning to see and development of eye, mind and hand coordination, and for encouraging selectivity. This exercise continues the opportunities for self-evaluation and discussion of many issues about drawing.

Methodology

Instructions are: Select several familiar objects and arrange on your desk as a small still life. Draw your composition in contour line with pencil. Points to remember on these exercises are to avoid tone and texture, to simplify detail and focus on surface as well as outline of the objects observed.

Variations for these contour line drawing exercises include: change of scale, such as drawing on a larger format or drawing objects larger or smaller than life size and change of media. For instance, drawing with felt pen and ink, or exploration of other subject matter.

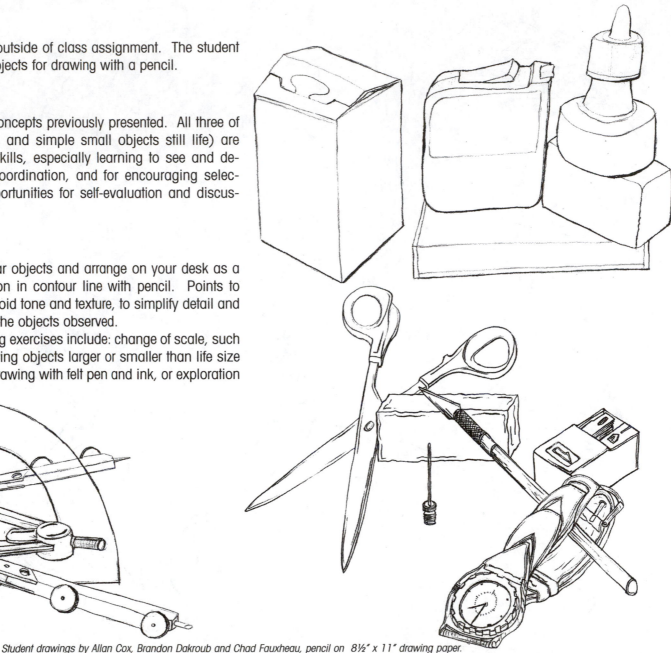

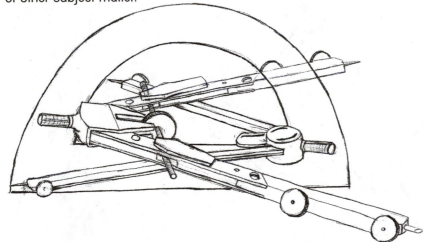

Student drawings by Allan Cox, Brandon Dakroub and Chad Fauxheau, pencil on 8½" x 11" drawing paper.

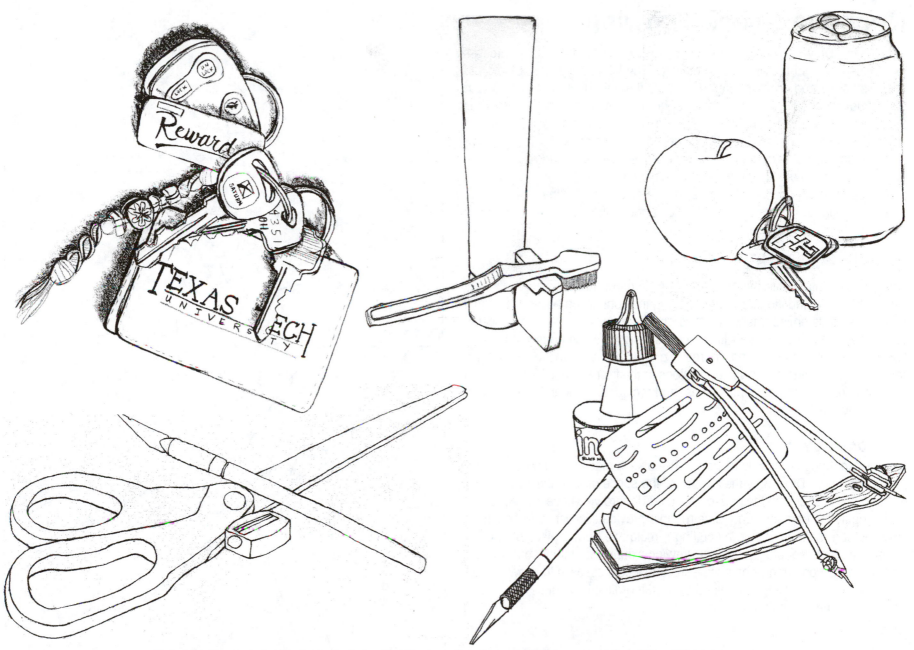

Student drawings by Amber Koenig, George Bailey, Ruel Mendoza, Chris Sturm and Ty Summers, pencil on 8½″ x 11″ drawing paper.

Negative Space Drawing

In her book, <u>Drawing on the Right Side of the Brain,</u> Betty Edwards addresses the concept of right brain/left brain activity. The left hemisphere of the brain controls verbal and analytic functions, while the right deals with spatial and perceptual processing. The premise is that by accessing both sides of the brain we can learn to "see," to perceive in ways necessary for artists and designers to function more effectively. Negative space drawing increases our ability to access both portions of the brain as we draw by enhancing creativity and confidence. It also is an effective tool for solving problems with perspective, proportion, shape and composition. Perception and manipulation of spaces in-between mass is essential for understanding the true nature of form.

Goals

This exercise introduces the concept of figure ground relationships, thereby establishing a foundation for understanding the connection between the built structure and its environment. It offers an opportunity to reinforce concepts covered with previous contour line exercises, such as line quality, composition and eye, mind and hand coordination with a more abstracted subject matter. Encouraging sensitive connections to the frame shape helps develop an awareness of compositional issues, and provides opportunity for analysis of eye movement.

Methodology

One student brings a bicycle to class. The bike is placed on a model stand. Instructions are: Draw only the shapes of the space around the form. Work within a frame shape on the paper. Use a cardboard viewfinder to help select and simplify the composition. Slide mounts provide excellent viewfinders or students can make their own by cutting a rectangle from a piece of opaque paper. Students should do several drawings during a single work session and compare work, analyzing successes and weaknesses in their own drawings. An added challenge is gained by working directly in ink.
derstanding the true nature of form.

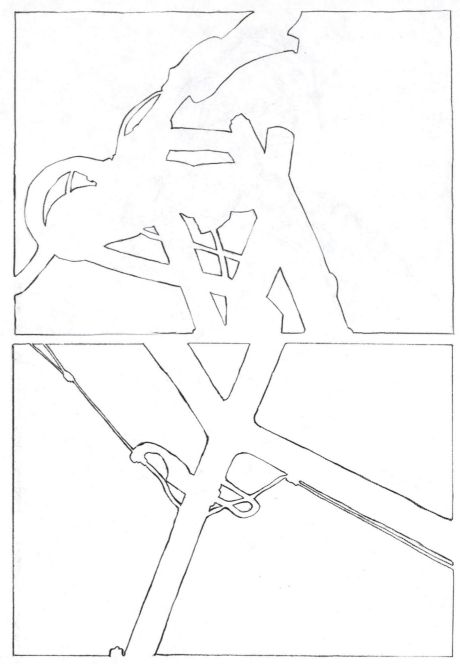

Student drawings by J. T. Unruh and Les Lawless, pencil on 8½" x 11" drawing paper.

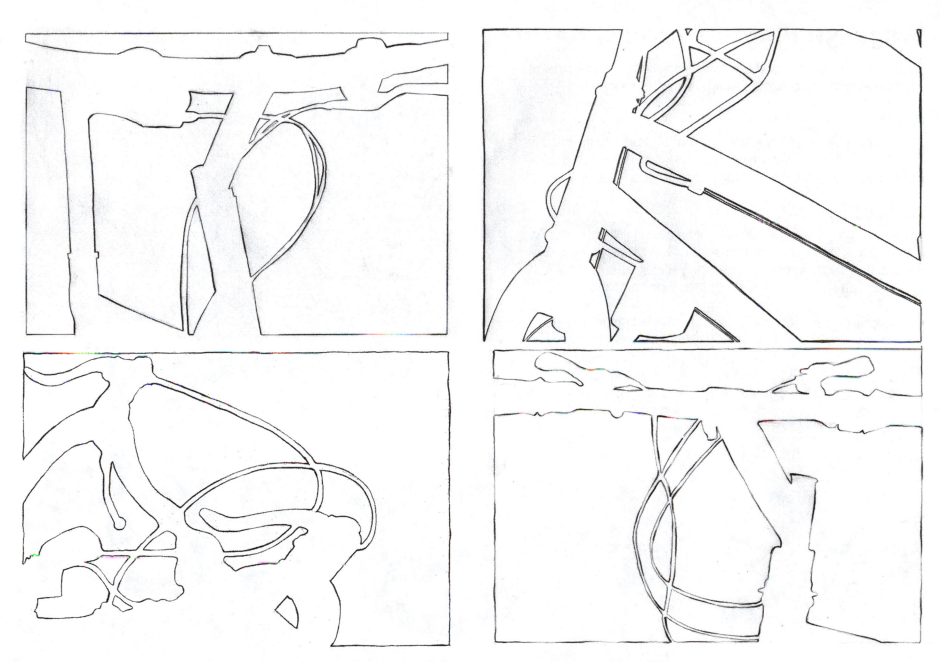

Student drawings by Wes Bowen, Daniel Pruske, Angela Jones and Chris Hodney, pencil on 8½″ x 11″ drawing paper.

13

Value Studies

The previous exercises used line to delineate form. These projects emphasize light and shadow as form builder rather than line.

Goals

Students develop sensitivity to value relationships in drawing through observation. There is also a continuation of the previous goal of developing a working understanding of figure ground relationships.

Methodology

Instructions for the first exercise are: Draw an egg without using any line. Observe the egg placed on a piece of white paper on your desk under a direct light source. Exaggerate dark tones, but do not lose white highlights. Look for the shadow core and reflected light.

Instructions for the second exercise are: Draw a crumpled paper sack. Observe the sack (or any stiff toned paper with folds crumpled into it) under a direct light source. Lightly sketch the structure of the form before developing light and dark values. Exaggerate the tonal relationships. These two exercises may be done in one class period or they may be given as a homework assignment.

Student drawings by Crystal Maeker, David Hastings, Brad Hackler, and Steven Couch on sketch paper, 8½" x 11".

14

Gray Marker Still Life Study

An extension of the value study of objects like eggs and paper sacks is the study of an arrangement of a variety of objects. For this project new media such as warm or cool gray markers are introduced. An alternative media is ink wash.

Goals

As students observe and explore the visual effects of various materials and textures they become more sensitive to their perceptions of value. A harmonious balance of form and value is desired throughout the whole composition.

Methodology

A complex still life arrangement is placed so the entire class is able to view it. If necessary, more than one set up may be placed at opposite ends of the classroom. Use a spotlight to produce more contrast of value relationships. Students are told to selectively crop their view of the arrangement to produce a pleasing composition within a frame shape. They are encouraged to use a cardboard viewfinder to help establish the basic composition. Rough thumbnail sketches in pencil are sometimes helpful in establishing a selective view. However, extensive pencil under-drawing is discouraged. Time should be allotted for several attempts. A preliminary demonstration of layering and blending with markers is useful.

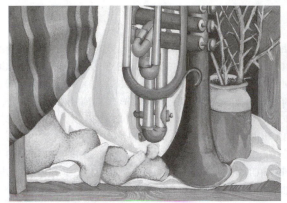

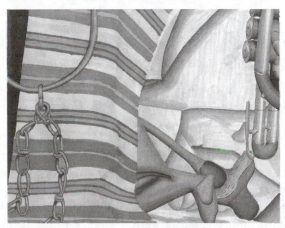

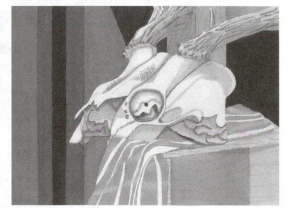

Student gray marker value studies by Crystal Maeker, Richard Gilland, Jason Darling, David Hastings, Michael Magee, Lauren Ford, and David Zabin

The Shoe

The study of familiar objects through drawing improves our visual acuity and skill in general graphic communication. Shoes provide a ready subject that is at once available and familiar and also presents diversity of form and character. Shoes can be studied with gestural line, reduced to geometric shapes, or viewed with accurate observation of positive and negative space. They can be explored in contour, cross contour and light and shade. Issues of composition are addressed through relationship of form to the space occupied. A shoe is an interesting vehicle for consideration of size, position and placement on the page. Further, this project continues potential for transition from gestural and contour line drawing to a more developed study involving tone and texture in a variety of media.

Goals

Students draw a more developed study, observing texture, value and form as an extension of an initial line drawing. They begin naturally to interconnect for purposeful expression the character of line with modeling.

Methodology

Instructions are: Place the shoe on the desk in front of you and try to draw life size. If possible, fit your shoe within an 8 ½" x 11" format. Sketch the form as a rapid gestural sketch, then work directly on top of your initial drawing and develop it as a more extended study. Correct proportion and perspective as you add detail without erasing your initial marks. Evaluate your work as it progresses. As a final step, weight the lines to communicate expression, rhythm, and solidity of form. Work on this drawing for at least one hour, gradually changing and adjusting the drawing as you observe.

For alternative exercises change the format, number of shoes in the composition and alter the media. Ink wash, pen and ink, charcoal or prisma pencils are good variations.

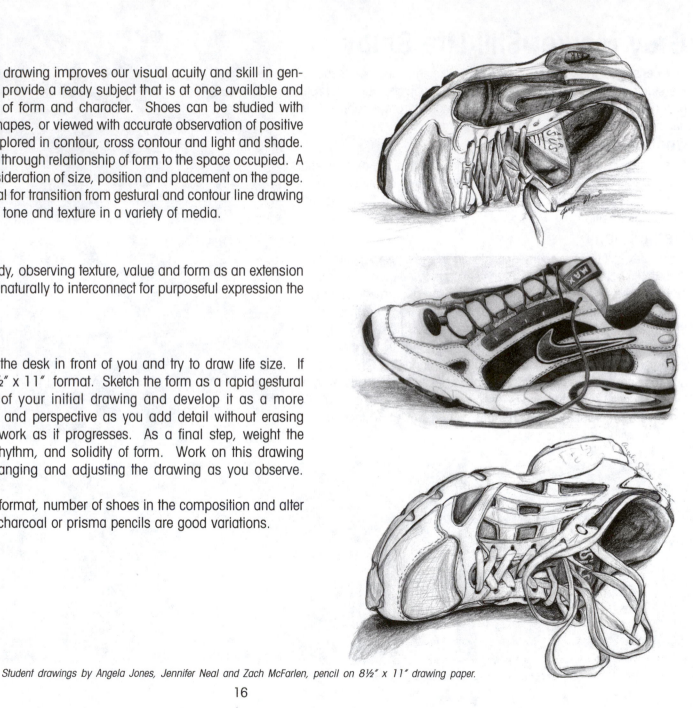

Student drawings by Angela Jones, Jennifer Neal and Zach McFarlen, pencil on 8½" x 11" drawing paper.

Student drawings, various sizes. Two shoes in pen and ink and in pencil by Jaime Gloe; shoes in ink wash by Ron Meyer; shoes by Ty Summers, Estaban Cantu, enise Judah, Loretta Lack and Daniel Pruske in pencil, all on drawing paper.

"Measured Drawing" of a Chair

Goals

Students increase skills of linear perspective; develop a sense of accurate proportion; and gain knowledge of and practice with a system that estimates the measurements in a perspective view.

Methodology

A chair is placed on a model stand in front of the class. Students are encouraged to "move in close," for better observation. Instructions are: Measure by sighting along your pencil. Hold pencil at arms length from your body. While holding your shoulders square to the picture plane, measure chair from intersecting points. Transfer these measurements to your paper and record points. Sketch lines between points. Use varied line weights and "turn corners". This assignment should be completed in two hours.

Student drawings by Zach McFarlen, B.J. Prichard, Daniel Pruske and Roaxanna Cummings, pencil on 8½" x 11" sketch paper.

Chair as Orthographic Projection

Various drawing systems provide a choice of alternative ways for communicating ideas. In design drawing especially, there are several alternatives. The most obvious way of drawing is simply an interpretation of what we see, providing us with an image similar to a camera view. Measurements and angles are usually estimated. This method provides information from a single point of view. Another type of drawing may provide a more detailed or complete picture by giving us multiple views of an object with exact measurements and angles. The latter drawing system more adequately tells how something is built. Various technical drawing systems are classified by method of projection or pictorial effect. Projection refers to the process of representing a three dimensional object by extending all its points in the form of straight lines to an imaginary transparent plane, called a picture plane. In orthographic projection, lines projected are parallel to one another and perpendicular to the picture plane. The result is a multi-view drawing that yields an image showing all sides. The most common use of this system is a plan view, elevations and or section. This type of drawing commonly is used by architects and designers for both design drawing and construction documents.

Goals

As a result of this experience, students increase their knowledge of the orthographic drawing process and increase their understanding of the basic concepts involved in multi-view and projection drawing.

Methodology

Prior to the beginning of student work, examples of plan, elevation and section drawings are shown in class and the concept of the "glass box" is explained. Students measure and record actual length from point to point on the chair that they drew in the "measured chair" project. The literal measurements are converted by means of an architect's scale to a drawing on translucent, blue lined grid paper as plan and elevations (top view, front view and side view) by means of orthographic projection. These drawings are then inked with technical pens.

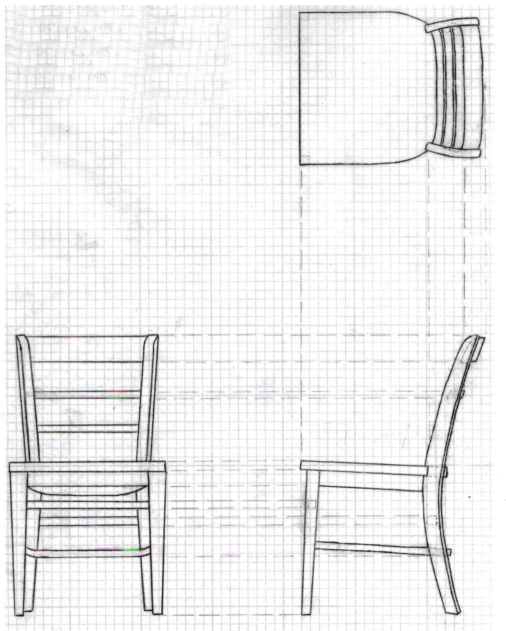

Student drawing by Zach McFarlen, ink on 11" x 17" translucent grid paper, 2 hours (with measuring and scaling).

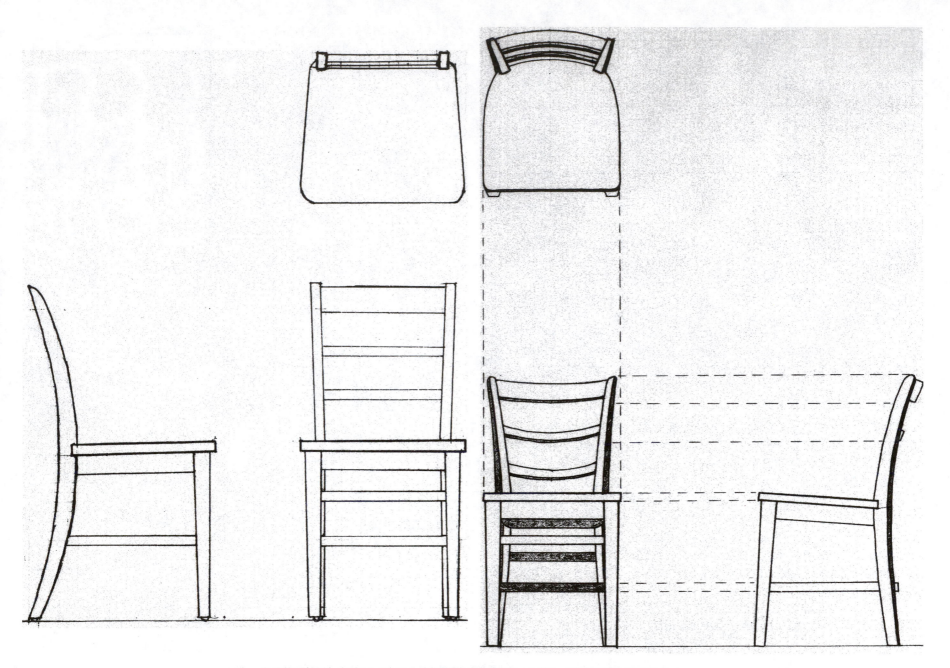

Student drawings by B. J. Prichard and Daniel Pruske, ink on 11″ x 17″ translucent grid paper.

20

Isometric Drawing with Shade and Projected Shadow

Goals

After this exercise students' drawings exhibit an understanding of principles of isometric construction, including shade and shadow casting. Their accuracy increases in visualization of three-dimensional objects. These mechanical shading skills later easily transfer to the renderings of complex architectural designs.

Methodology

Students are instructed by means of a demonstration how to construct a basic cube as an isometric paraline drawing. Basic principles of shade and shadow casting, using a horizontal angle of bearing and a 45° angle of altitude, are demonstrated. Prepared handouts that describe principles of isometric construction and shadow casting in paraline drawing, in plan and elevation are distributed. If time permits, a cardboard model is constructed prior to the shadow casting process and observed under a controlled light source. Axonometric shade and shadow work sheets demonstrating solutions to specific configurations are helpful. Students work on translucent vellum grid paper with drafting equipment. They develop original, increasingly complex architectonic compositions. Presentation drawings are done by tracing in freehand over the initial constructions in pen and ink. Students draw the object they design from the opposite side in isometric, in plan view and elevation. Following this exercise a skills exam to test retention of principles and process is given.

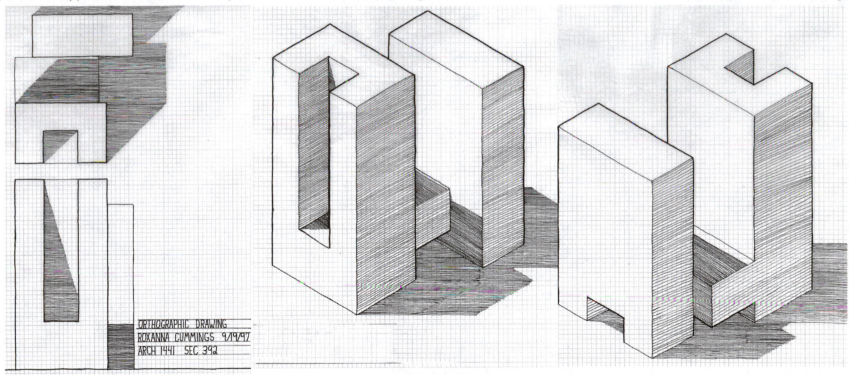

Student drawing by Roxanna Cummings, technical pen and ink on 11" x 17" translucent grid paper.

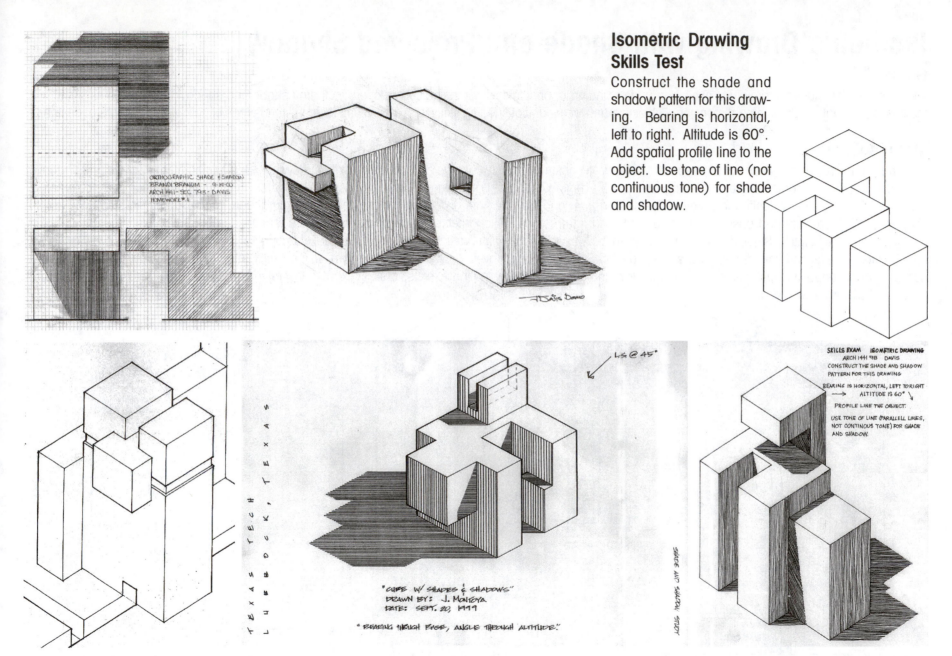

Isometric Drawing Skills Test

Construct the shade and shadow pattern for this drawing. Bearing is horizontal, left to right. Altitude is 60°. Add spatial profile line to the object. Use tone of line (not continuous tone) for shade and shadow.

Student orthographic drawing with shade and shadow cast by Brandi Branum, class demo drawing by J. Davis , student skills exam solution, exemplary student isometric shade and shadow presentation by Jaime Montoya, class demo of an imaginary isometric architectonic creation for shade and shadow practice by J. Davis, all drawings ink on tracing paper, 8½" x 11".

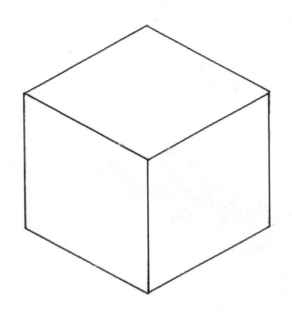

Typical Problems

Construct the shade and shadow patterns for each of these isometric drawings. Completed solutions on reverse.

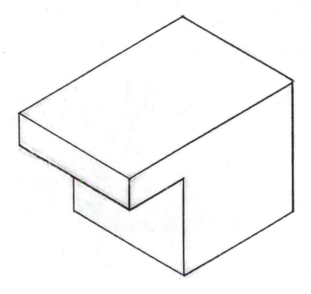

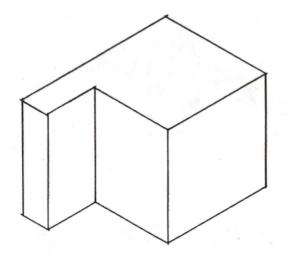

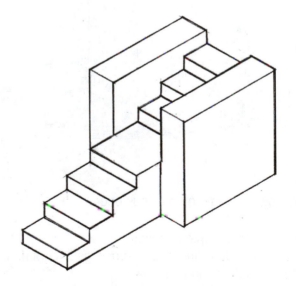

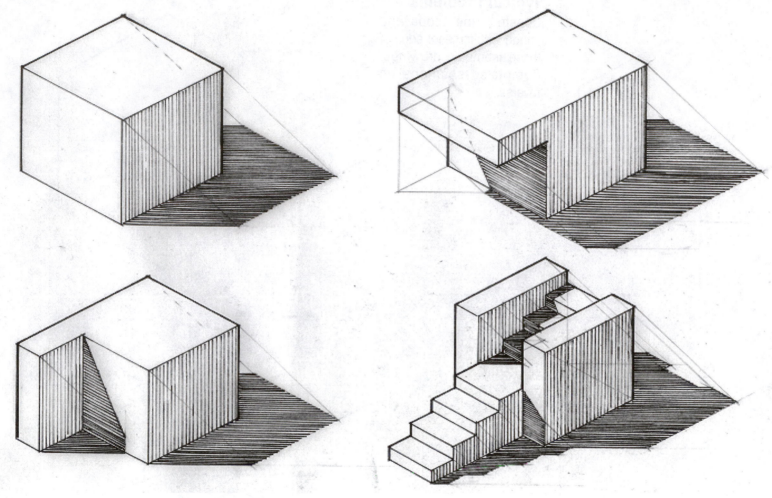

Solutions

to shade and shadow problems on previous page.

Notes:

* Always be aware of turning corners.
* Use spatial profile lines in paraline drawings to communicate volume.
* Cast shadow is darker than shade.
* Don't draw outline (object line around cast shadow.
* Direction of line in shading follows primary direction of the plane on which it falls, i.e. on horizontal surface use horizontal lines for shadow, etc.

24

Multiple Vanishing Points

In a perspective drawing, objects get smaller as they recede in space and receding parallel lines merge toward a vanishing point on the horizon line. Objects that have different alignments in the same pictorial plane will have different vanishing points. In this case multiple vanishing points will exist in the same pictorial space.

Goals

The goal of this exercise is to create a better understanding of perspective drawing. As a study in value, this exercise challenges the student to become more aware of subtle changes in value and texture.

Methodology

Create a still life made of various objects turned at different angles. This will create a multiple vanishing point situation. All studies are done in black and white media (ink, graphite, ink wash and gray marker). Emphasis should be placed on obtaining a large range of value. A ten part value scale is drawn to encourage the student to employ a large range of value when drawing the still life.

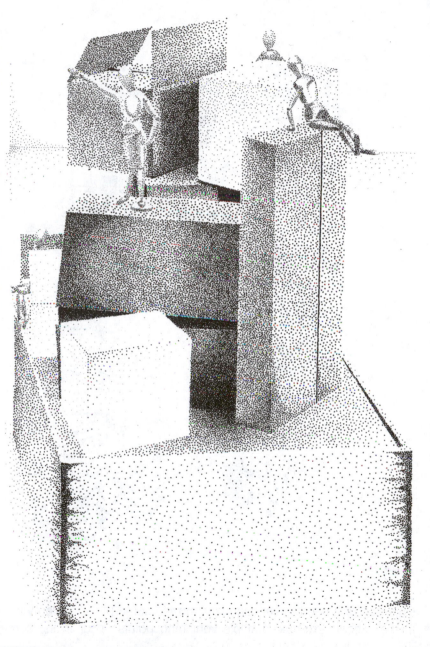

Student drawings by David Hastings, gray marker on sketch paper and by Anthony Lee, pen and ink on sketch paper.

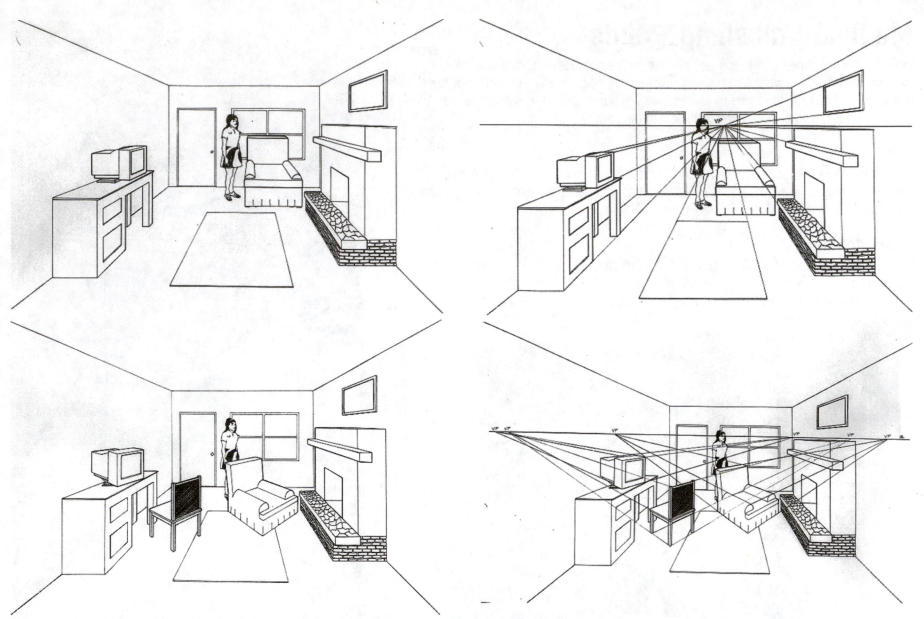

Objects that have different alignments in the same pictorial plan will have different vanishing points. In the first example, there is a single vanishing point, in the second example multiple vanishing points occur in the same pictorial space.

Student drawings by Tony Saenz, ink on vellum.

Still Life Emphasizing Visual Unity

An essential element of visual unity is that the whole must prevail over the sum of its parts. Individual elements must consciously be organized so that the whole creates a unified design. The concept of visual unity forms the foundation for all design disciplines. Even a work of art with pleasant subject matter and technical proficiency may produce a feeling of aversion if the sum of its parts are arranged poorly.

Goals

In this assignment the student's goal is to see the composition as a whole, rather than simply a collection of unrelated elements.

Methodology

On a sheet of 9″ x 12″ drawing paper, each student must create four different compositions using four or more objects. The composition should be based on principles of design for visual harmony as illustrated on page 60. Each student should produce four individual drawings using four different media (ink, graphite, wash and gray marker). Each drawing should illustrate one or more principle of visual harmony, for example: repetition, rhythm, continuation or proximity.

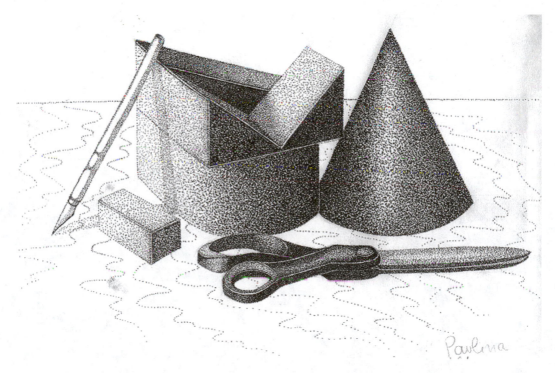

Student drawing by Pavlina Ilieva, pen and ink on sketch paper.

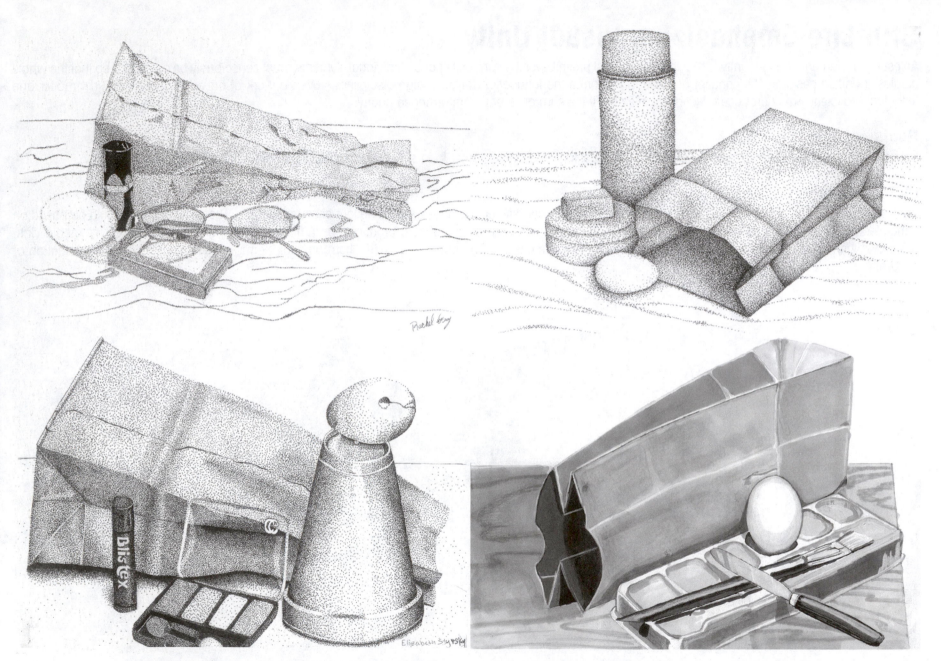

Student drawings by Rachel Fry, Amanda Schulte, Elizabeth Styrsky, pen and ink on sketch paper and by Carla Booth, gray marker on sketch paper.

28

White on Black

With the egg and sack value studies, form resulted from the addition and manipulation of shade. In this project, form is developed by building areas of light. Drawing in this manner requires thoughtful analysis of the reflectivity of surfaces.

Goals

Students develop increased sensitivity to the relationship between texture, pattern and value. Skill is increased through observation and analysis, and the importance of value relationships to composition becomes more apparent.

Methodology

A relatively complex, large still life is set up for the entire class to use. Various themes such as building technology (with tools and materials) or western (with ropes, boots, hat and spurs) may be presented to encourage unity in the design statement. A spotlight facilitates strong shadows. Instructions are: Focus on a part of the still life rather than trying to draw the entire arrangement. Selectively crop the composition. Make preliminary rough sketches in pencil on white sketch paper to develop the composition before starting to draw on the black board. Use black museum board and white prisma color pencils as media for the finished project.

An interesting variation to this project is to use gray board and work with black and white wax pencils. The same still life is appropriate for exploration with other media such as ink wash or pen and ink.

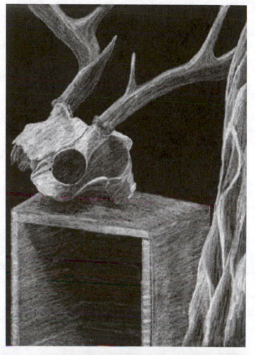

Student drawings by Christopher Davison, Emily Morris, David Zabin, David Hastings, Crystal Maeker, white prisma pencil on black museum board.

Complex Still Life

The technique is drawing directly with pen and ink. Initially this project intimidates some students because of its immediacy and permanency. Ink does not erase as easily as pencil. Most students view this project as a new challenge.

Goals

Students increase skills of free hand drawing with pen and ink. They discern from the apparent clutter of a complex arrangement the essentials of a dynamic composition. They abstract and manipulate parts of the arrangement to create visual interest, and they develop skills in manipulation of value and tactile relationships.

Methodology

Instructions are: Observe and mentally compose a picture before starting to draw. Use a viewing frame to crop for composition. Lightly sketch or block in the arrangement and general proportion of objects. Media include crow quill pens and/or technical drawing pens of various point sizes. A strong light source helps to cast shadows and define lights and darks.

Student drawing by Brad Hackler, pen and ink on 8½" x 11" drawing paper.

30

Figure Studies

In presentation drawings, nothing communicates scale better than the human figure. Architects and designers use figures to add life and activity to their presentations. People in a drawing inform the viewer of the function or purpose of the built form. Subconsciously the addition of scaled figures causes the observer to identify with the project. People in the drawing make it easier for the client to mentally put himself or herself into the proposed environment. The ability to sketch scale figures is an asset for the designer at the initial stages of designing. A figure helps one to visualize true space and proportion while designing.

Human beings have drawn people since Paleolithic times. Although the human figure was evident throughout the history of art, many students feel intimidated or uncomfortable at first when asked to draw a person. Tracing figures from an entourage file is quick and easy, but without a familiarity with the human body, traced figures often appear stilted and amateurish. If students have the opportunity, they need to take a life drawing class to learn more about anatomy and the animation of the human figure. The following exercises do not replace a life drawing class, but they do help students make more confident and successful application of figures to architectural presentations. Individuals who learn to successfully draw the human figure can observe and draw most any other object.

Goals

Students develop a heightened sense of proportion, rhythm and balance through direct observation of the human figure while drawing. By means of the experience they are able to use tracing files with more expression and vitality and their application of entourage figures becomes more believable.

Methodology

For a unit on figure drawing students take turns as models for a variety of life drawing exercises as follows:

Gesture drawing — Students draw as freely and quickly as possible to capture a first impression. Gesture drawing captures movement, action and balance. This is a good way to "loosen up" at the start of each day's lesson of life drawing activities.

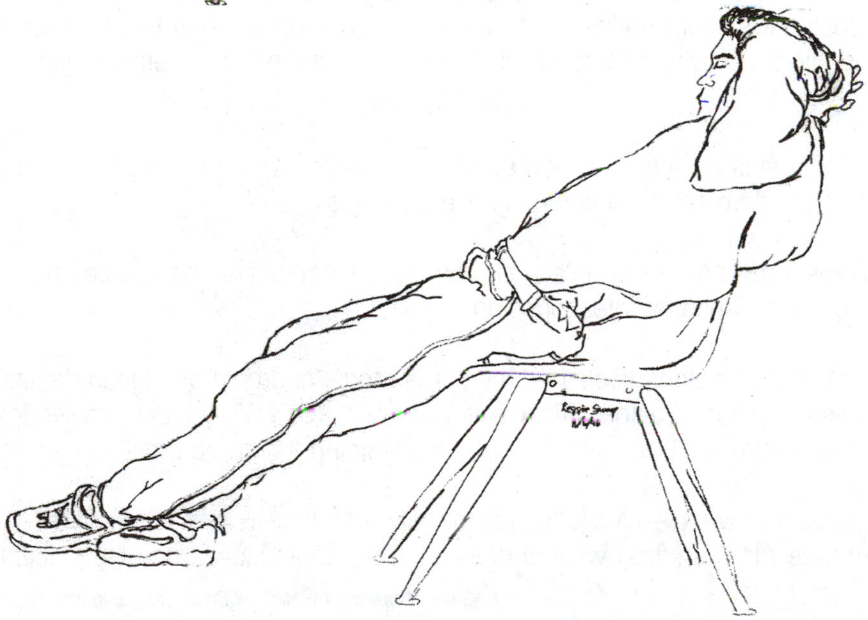

Student drawings by Michael Bryan and Reggie Savage, 18" x 24", pencil on sketch paper.

31

Timed gesture drawing — Start by allowing students 15 minutes to draw a figure, then 10 minutes, 5 minutes, 2 minutes, 1 minute, 30 seconds. Six gesture drawings of figures done in this sequence provide an intense experience that communicates the nature of gesture. Students learn to capture the moment.

Contour line drawing — This activity is a transition from earlier basic drawing activities. It is a good idea to vary the scale, encourage students to draw large and fill the area of a large sketchpad (18" x 24" or larger).

Extended studies — Students are allowed one hour or more to complete a figure study. This presents opportunities to explore tone and detail.

Portraits — Although designers may not have many occasions to draw portraits, knowledge of accurate proportion in the human face can make simplified scale figures more believable. Many students are reluctant to draw faces, therefore when success is achieved, it is a great confidence builder. A variation to this activity is for students to draw a self-portrait while looking in a mirror.

Multi-figures — Students draw the model in class and add to this composition from photographs or entourage files. In another version of this activity, the model takes different poses while the student builds a single composition with several views of the same person. An additional activity is to add environment from magazines or entourage files to their life drawings.

People sketchbook — A homework assignment is to draw a person a day in a notebook. This builds a personal entourage file of figures.

Foreshortening -- Students work from the model at extreme angles and exaggerate the illusion of distance by foreshortening.

Drawing at various scales -- The same model is drawn at various architectural scales with different levels of detail. A figure drawn at ½" = 1'- 0" includes greater detail than the same figure drawn at 1/8" = 1'- 0" while maintaining the same proportions.

Memory drawing — A challenging activity is for the students to observe the model for a period of time (10 minutes) without drawing. The model leaves and the students draw the figure

Student drawing by Michael Bryan (top) and class demonstration drawing by J. Davis, 18" x 24", pencil on sketch paper.

Class demonstration drawings by J. Davis, (left) and student drawings by Ruel Mendoza and Chris Sturm, pencil on 8½" x 11" drawing paper.

33

Quick Sketch Studies of the Human Figure

Drawing exercises that involve quick sketch studies of the human figure helps to develop a more accurate way of seeing. The figure is used as a model for achieving greater understanding of form. These studies may be used to create a personal text for entourage authenticity.

James C. Watkins, quick sketch figure studies for authentic entourage, ink, ebony pencil, and ink wash.

34

Adult Proportions

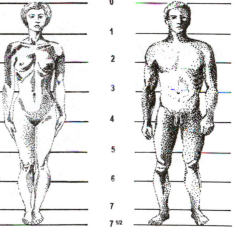

Shoulders at 1 1/3 heads
Elbows at 3 heads
Navel at 3 heads
Crotch at 4 heads
Fingertips at 4 1/2 heads
Knees at 5 1/2 heads

James C. Watkins, quick sketch figure studies for authentic entourage, ink and ebony pencil.

Tree Sketchbook

Landscape elements add scale, life and realism to an architectural rendering. Background trees define a building form and foreground trees help to frame a composition. The type of foliage delineated gives context to a site, provides a compositional accent to the built form and may determine a color scheme for the rendering.

Goals

Drawing from nature develops observational and interpretive skills. A sketchbook gives the student a ready reference file for entourage application.

Methodology

This is a homework assignment. Instructions are: Draw a tree a day from observation. Sketch in different media, styles and techniques. Draw close up views of limbs and leaves, groups of trees in the distance, different plant forms such as cacti, and house plants, trees in conjunction with other landscape elements, and extended studies of individual tree types. At the end of three weeks, turn in a sketchbook with approximately 20 pages of tree drawings.

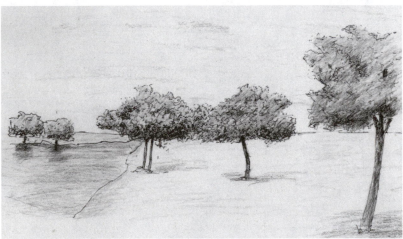

Student Drawings by Amber Storer, Scott Snyder, Jose Chavez, Matt Stevens.

36

Student tree sketchbook drawings by Ryan Bemberg, Amber Dawn Storer, David Hastings, Matt Stevens, and Kirk Klatt, various media and sizes.

Field Sketching

For many people the camera has replaced the sketchbook. However, Bryan Edwards argues in his book, <u>Understanding Architecture through Drawing</u>, that freehand drawing helps one to understand architecture and to develop visual sensitivity and awareness of design. There is a long tradition of observing and studying architecture through drawing. Field drawing from direct observation is both rewarding and challenging.

Goals

By visually exploring and developing sensitivity to the environment around us, students grow as artists and designers. Both sketching and analytical drawing give them a means of understanding form and construction. Visual images are catalogued in the mind for future inspiration.

Methodology

Instructions are: Take your sketchbooks, go on discovery walks and field trips whenever possible. Draw commercial and residential buildings, historic structures, and construction sites. Look for good composition and include entourage elements for scale and activity. Sketch in a variety of media. Use pencil, pen and ink, and felt marker.

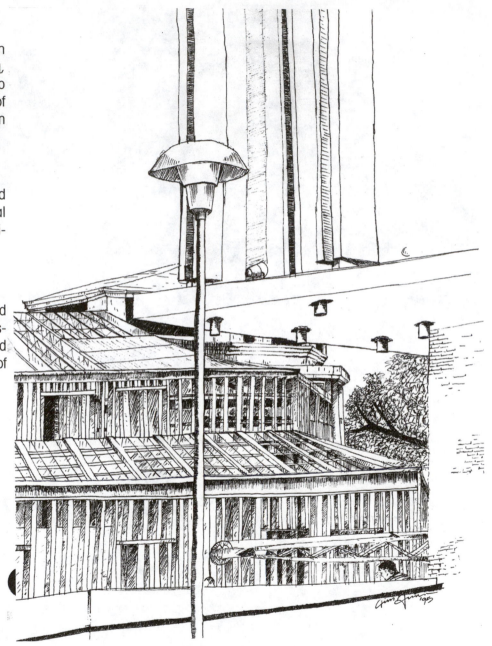

Student drawings by José Maese and Jim Gunn, pen and ink on 11" x 14"drawing paper.

38

Student drawings by Ruel Mendoza, Jamie Smith, Ty Summers and Brad Hackler, various sizes and media.

Parallel Perspective

Essential drawing experiences for potential architects and designers are those that focus on principles of perspective. A good introduction starts with one point or parallel perspective. The following two assignments are presented simultaneously to show students the relationship between simply drawing what we see and a mechanical method of constructing a perspective drawing. The subject for the first assignment is a hallway in the classroom building. This is an observational drawing done in class under the instructor's supervision. The second is a homework assignment. Students use a grid method with measurements taken from a bedroom off campus as a resource. The first assignment is an extended drawing in pencil and the second is drawn on vellum in pencil and traced in pen and ink for the final product.

Goals

Students learn to use two methods of drawing a perspective – a free hand "measured drawing" and a specific grid method. They develop an understanding of the process and principles of both types of perspective along with an increased confidence in their ability to produce a basic perspective drawing. They start to appreciate entourage elements such as plants, people and furnishings along with the basic architectural structure.

Methodology (hall)

Instructions are: Draw on site and use sketching skills as a means to study the environment. Position yourself facing square to a wall in front of you, viewing the length of a hall. Keep advancing walls perpendicular to your plane of vision. Measure the wall you are facing by sighting along your pencil as demonstrated*. Transfer those measurements to the center of your paper. In order to make accurate estimated measurements keep your shoulders square, your pencil parallel to the picture plane and held at arm's length. Sketch the wall facing you according to the estimated measurements. Locate the horizon line and vanishing point (relative to your position) and sketch the diagonals through the corners from the vanishing point. In the same manner, measure the advancing walls against the imaginary picture plane. Sketch freehand but check your measured lines against a straight edge. Maintain all vertical and horizontal lines and make sure all diagonals recede to a common vanishing point. Continue sketching lightly in this manner until you have captured the structure of the

Student hallway drawing by José Chavez, pencil on 18" x 24" drawing paper.

40

architecture. Add shading to "turn corners." Continue to develop detail in texture, reflections and cast shadows. Strive for good composition, variety of line quality, and use of tone. Add human figures for scale and activity. The completed drawing will appear somewhat sketchy and spontaneous while maintaining a sense of correct proportion and controlled drawing.

*At the start of this project the instructor gives a brief demonstration for the class, measuring and sketching the structure and demonstrating texture and value applications without completing a finished drawing. Also, the grid project has a demonstration accompanied by a handout showing the incremental steps. It is helpful to display examples of similar drawings and discuss their attributes before students actually start to draw.

Student drawings by, Roxanna Cummings, Ruel Mendoza and Corey Cash, pencil on 18" x 24", drawing paper, one week of class time (up to 8 hours).

Student hallway drawing by Daniel Pruske, pencil on 18" x 24" drawing paper.

Methodology (room)

A drawing of a dorm room or a room at home is constructed by transposing measurements of the room and furnishings to scale onto a constructed perspective grid of the space. This process requires a series of transparent overlays on tracing paper, including grid, composition, detail and final rendering in ink.

Instructions: Measure your room. Draw an elevation of the wall your are facing to scale (1/4″ = 1′ 0″ or 1/2″ = 1′ 0″ depending on the size of the room). The maximum size of this drawing is 11″ x 14″. Determine the horizon line and vanishing point (your eye level while standing will establish an appropriate horizon line for the addition of a human figure to represent yourself in your room.) Lightly mark in 1″ increments to scale around the perimeter of the wall. From the vanishing point, draw through these measured marks. This establishes the vanishing lines for your grid. Measure, using scale, from the vanishing point along the horizon line to the near side , the distance to your station point. A good rule of thumb to determine this measurement for an averaged proportioned rectilinear space is one and one half times the width of the back wall. This distance will provide you with a measuring point from which you can draw through the near corner and by way of subsequent receding lines to establish square feet vanishing or advancing on the grid. Connect points established with vertical and horizontal lines to complete the grid. Use the grid on the floor to establish a footprint for furnishings and establish heights to a relative scale by moving horizontally along the grid to a side wall and then vertically up the wall to the correct height measurement and then back to the object.

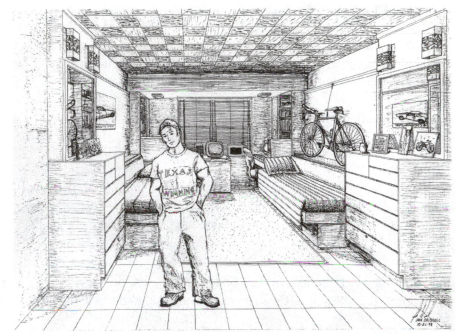

Student drawings by John Drisoll and Loretta Lack, pen and ink on 11″ x 17″ transparent grid paper, two-week homework assignment (8 hours).

Two-Point Perspectives with Entourage

In architectural drawing the function of entourage and perspectives is essential. This combination offers the most realistic view of all the pictorial graphics. The addition of entourage adds an element of believability. When creating a perspective drawing with entourage the location of the horizon line becomes vital in determining the scale and view seen by the observer. Therefore, a conscious decision must be made regarding the height of the horizon line.

The true horizon line is always eye level to the observer. The horizon line will cross all planes at 5 ½' when an observer measuring 6' is standing eye level to the horizon line. In this case all standing adult figures on the same level with the observer must be placed eye level or near eye level to the horizon line to be compatible with the scale of the building.

When the horizon line is below or above a standing figure (meaning, when the observer is elevated above or stooped below other standing figures) a scaled measurement must be taken of the height of a person. This measurement could come from a doorway or the corner of a building. The measurement is then taken to both vanishing points and extended out. Scaled figures may then be placed between these extended lines (as shown in the illustrations).

Goals

The goal is to learn how to draw two-point perspectives, and how to include scaled entourage to create a convincing environment. This exercise also teaches students how to place scaled figures in a drawing regardless of the height of the horizon line.

Methodology

On site studies of historical residential buildings are used as a subject. These buildings are chosen because of their intimate scale and rich texture. All studies are done in black and white media (ink, graphite, wash and gray marker).

Student drawing by Geoffrey Harral, ink on 20" x 30" tracing paper.

44

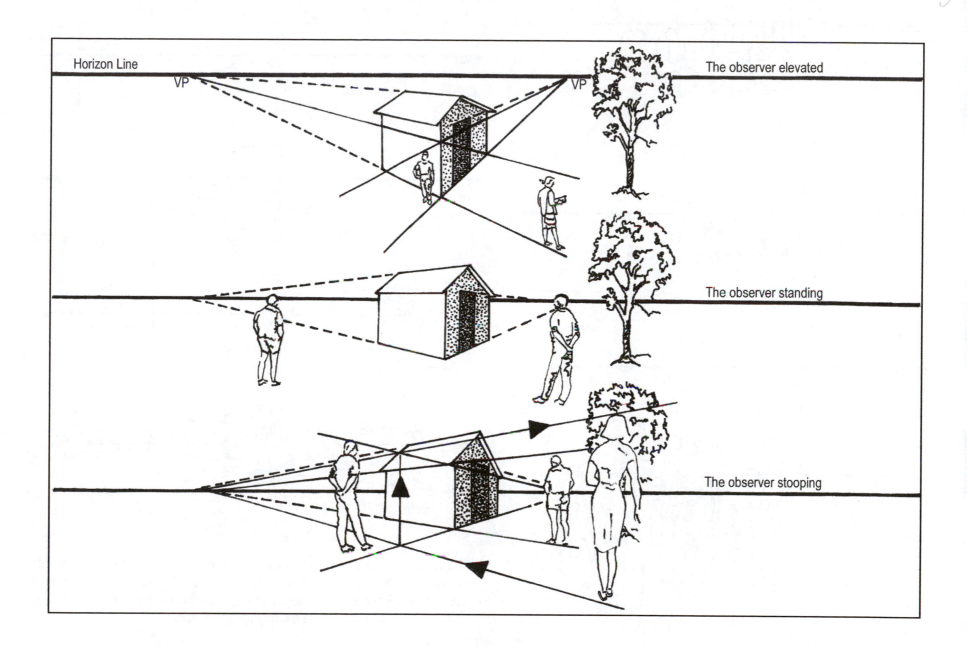

Horizon Line

VP

VP

The observer elevated

The observer standing

The observer stooping

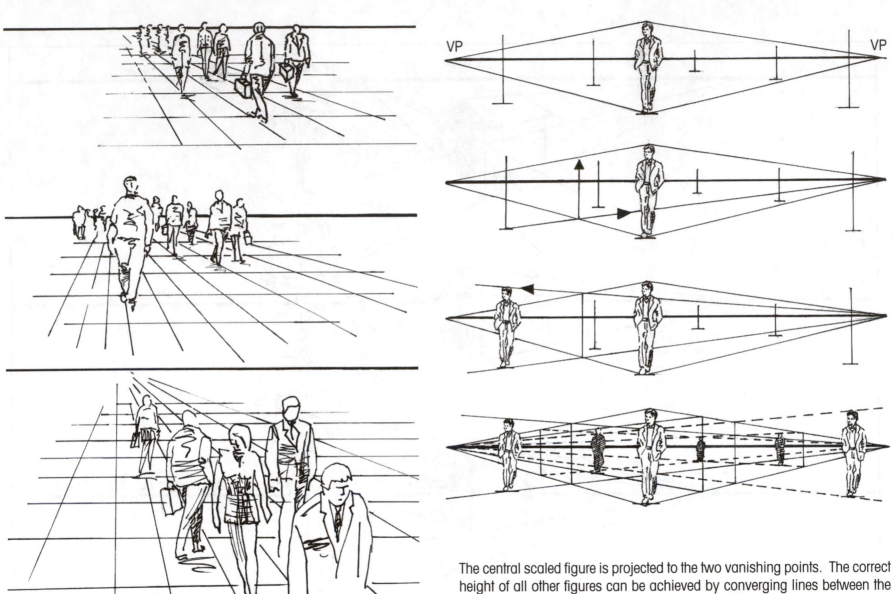

The central scaled figure is projected to the two vanishing points. The correct height of all other figures can be achieved by converging lines between the vanishing point lines of the central figure. This creates a situation where all figures are at the same scale as they recede in space.

Student drawing by Josh Koch and Brock Bejcek, ink on 18" x 24" drawing paper.

47

Student drawings by Stephen Martinez, gray marker on 18" x 24" drawing paper and Student drawing by Kim Drake, ink on18" x 24" drawing paper. Student drawings by William Evan Figueroa, graphite on 18" x 24' drawing paper and Student drawing by Sze-Lyn Lim, ink wash on 18" x 24" drawing paper.

Entourage demonstration sketches by J. Davis, various sizes and media.

49

Lettering
Block Vertical Capitals

1. Major titles should be 1/4" high.
2. Minor title should be 3/16" high.
3. The minimum height of any lettering is 1/8" high.

ABCDEFGHIJKLMNOPQRSTUVWXYZ

1234567890

ABCDEFGHIJKLMNOPQRSTUVWXYZ

1234567890

ABCDEFGHIJKLMNOPQRSTUVWXYZ

1234567890

DRAWING USES A KIND OF UNIVERSAL LANGUAGE. THE WORD "DRAW" MEANS TO DRAG A POINTED INSTURMENT SUCH AS A PEN, PENCIL, OR BRUSH OVER A SMOOTH SURFACE, LEAVING BEHIND THE MARKS OF ITS PASSAGE. THE SCRIBBLES OF CHILDREN ARE DRAWINGS AS TRULY AS ARE THE SKETCHES OF THE MASTERS. CHILDREN MAKE MARKS ON SURFACES LONG BEFORE THEY LEARN TO WRITE. IT IS EASY TO UNDERSTAND, THEREFORE, THAT DRAWING IS THE MOST FUNDAMENTAL OF THE ARTS AND IS CLOSELY RELATED TO ALL THE OTHERS. WRITING ITSELF IS SIMPLY THE DRAWING OF LETTERS, WHICH ARE SYMBOLS FOR SOUNDS. (COMPTON'S ENCYCLOPEDIA)

Graphic Symbols

Graphic symbols are designed to give information about size and direction. They should be kept simple and at a moderate size in order to be understood easily and should not overpower a presentation drawing. There are standards for appropriate use of line weight and type. The standard way of using lines and symbols is referred to as convention. When everyone in the profession uses a standard convention they are using the same visual vocabulary.

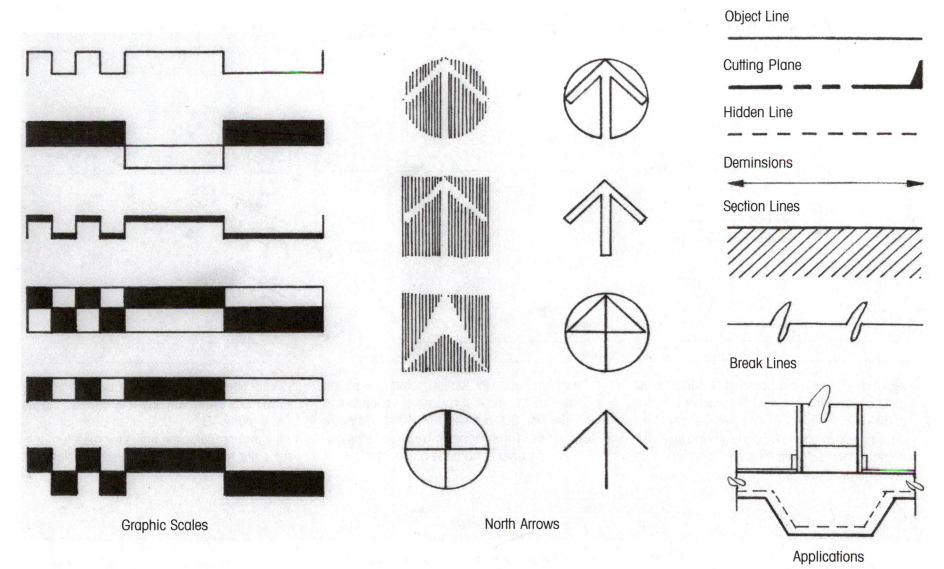

Object Line

Cutting Plane

Hidden Line

Deminsions

Section Lines

Break Lines

Graphic Scales

North Arrows

Applications

Creating a Two-Point Perspective Using the Plan Projection Method

The plan projection method (known as "office or common method") is used to create a three-dimensional illusion of objects and buildings from the accurate dimensions of plans and elevations.

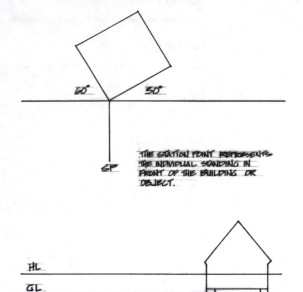

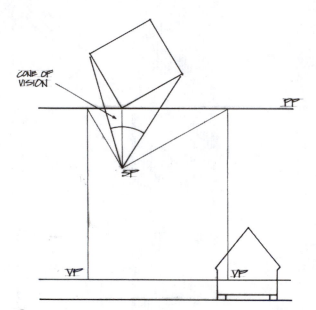

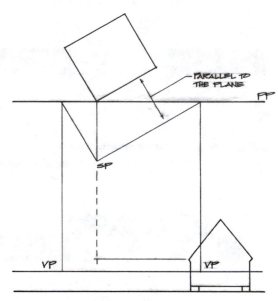

1 Place a corner of your object or building on the picture plane line. Orient the object or building at 60 - 30° or 45° - 45° for convenience. Draw an elevation to one side on the ground line. The horizon line is drawn to scale, measuring up from the ground line.

2 Select and locate the station point. The station point should be set at a cone of vision that is greater than 30° but less than 60° to minimize distortions. The station point represents the distance the viewer is from the object at scale.

3 Draw lines from the station point, parallel to two faces of the plan until they intersect the picture plane. Bring those lines down at 90° to the picture plane line until they meet the horizon line to establish the vanishing points.

Student drawings by Jaime Montoya, pen and ink on vellum.

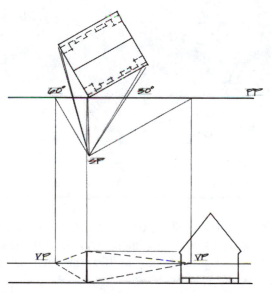

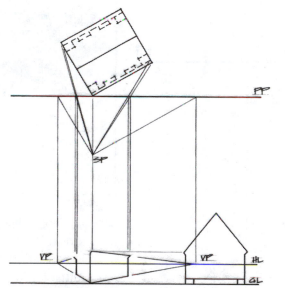

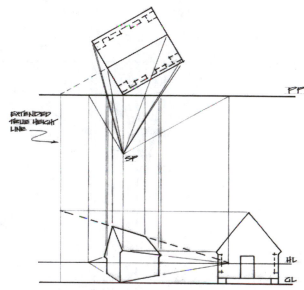

4 The corner of the plan that touches the picture plane represents the true height. The true height of objects can be determined by bringing a line down from the corner that touches the picture plane line to the ground line. The true height can be determined via the elevation.

5 Make a line from the station point to all corners of the plan. When the lines cross the picture plane line, bring the line down until they intersect with the receding lines merging toward the vanishing points.

6 Any corner or edge can be turned into a true height line by extending a line out until it meets the picture plane line. When this line meets the picture plane line bring it down to meet the ground line. Take the extended true height line to the vanishing point until it intersects with its projected lines.

Student drawings by Jaime Montoya, pen and ink on vellum.

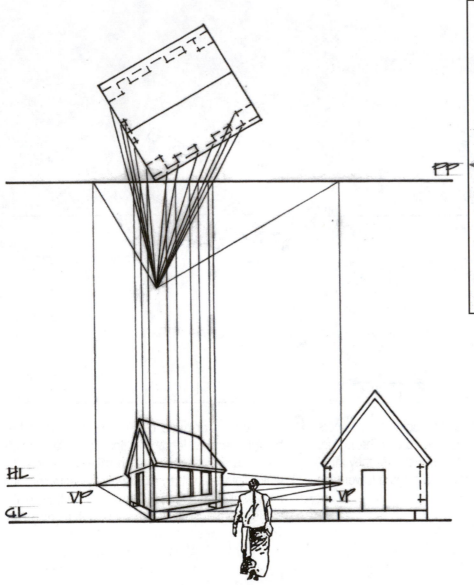

7 All hidden lines must be drawn on the plan in order to project them down to the intersecting vanishing point lines. The horizon line is measured to scale from the ground line. In this case, five feet in order to place figures eye level to the horizon line.

PP

HL

VP

VP

GL

Axonometric Drawing

Axonometric drawing also called "paraline drawing" includes isometrics, plan obliques, and elevation obliques. Axonometric drawing is a form of pictorial graphics that show three faces of an object in one orthographic view: Parallel lines remain parallel to each other.

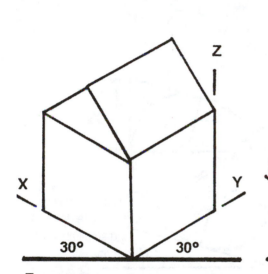

1 Isometric

Isometric drawings are drawn at 30°-30° with all three faces having equal emphasis. The X. Y. Z axes are drawn to the same scale.

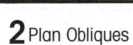

2 Plan Obliques

Plan obliques are drawn at 45°-45° or 60°-30° which utilizes the orthographic plan. The plan oblique has a higher angle than an isometric. Therefore, the X, Y and Z-axes are not always equal. The Z-axis may be scaled down when distortion is objectionable.

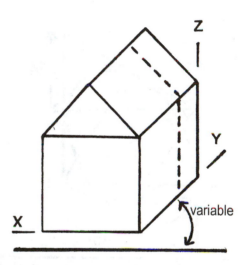

3 Elevation obliques

Elevation obliques show the face of the building or object (to scale) parallel to the drawing surface. Elevation obliques utilizes the orthographic elevation. The Y-axis may appear distorted. Therefore, the X., Y, and Z-axes are not always equal. The Y axis may be scaled down when distortion is objectionable.

Axonometric Circles

Axonometric circles appear as ellipses. The process of creating circles in paraline drawings is called "the four-center ellipse method".

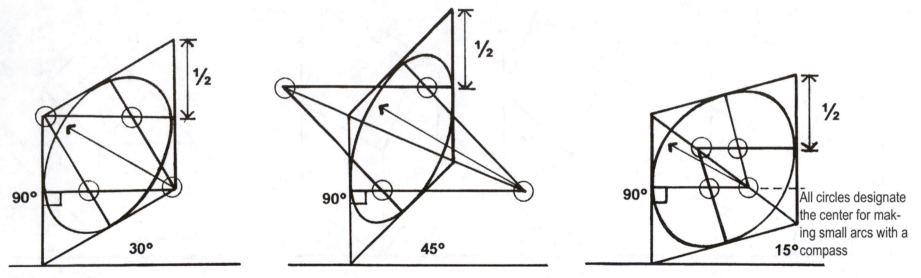

Construction

A paraline square must be drawn. Find the midpoints on both vertical sides of the square. Next, draw perpendicular lines from the two mid-points. In an isometric square these lines will intersect at the corner of the square. The four intersecting points form the arc-centers. Complete small arcs with a compass from the arc-centers to form the ellipse. To form an ellipse from an oblique square the same process is repeated with the addition of a diagonal line that is drawn through the center of the square. The four intersecting points form the arc-centers.

A Circle in Perspective

A circle in perspective appears as an ellipse. The method for creating a perspective circle is called "the twelve point method".

All small circles designate points which are connected to form a circle. A flexible curve may be used to connect the points to create the elipse.

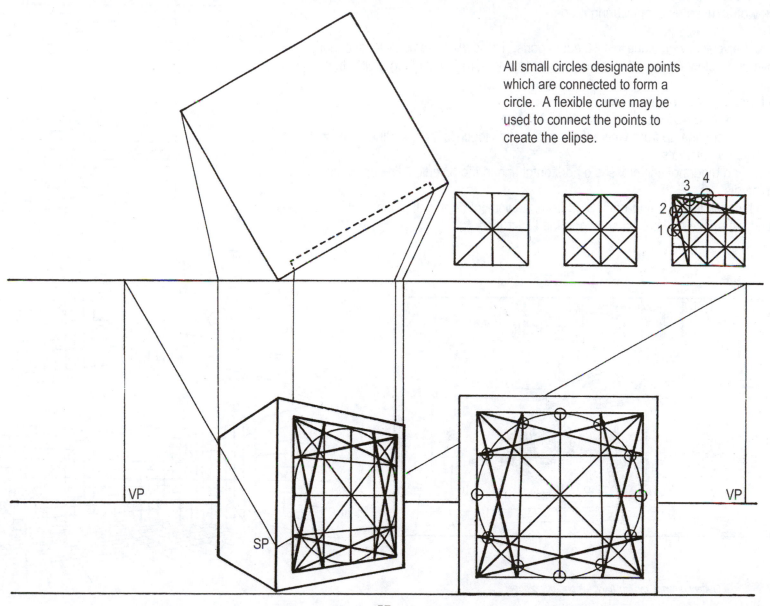

Two-Point Perspective Grid

These steps explain how to create a two-point perspective grid. In a two-point perspective grid the back wall is used as a measuring plane.

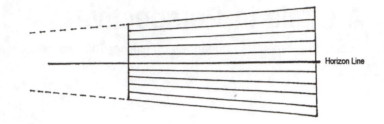

Horizon Line

(1)   Divide the vertical wall plane into 10 equal parts. These measurements taper equally above and below the horizon line as they merge toward a vanishing point off the page.

(2)   The horizon line is on the 5' line.

(3)   Draw a line at a 45° angle up from 0' to 10' line.

(4)   Take a vertical line up from where the diagonal line touches the floor line. This will give you 10' intervals.

(5)   Wherever a diagonal line crosses a horizontal line, bring a vertical line up to create 1' intervals.

(6)   Place the visible vanishing point 3' in from the vertical right wall plane.

(7)   Extend the space forward as shown in the illustration.

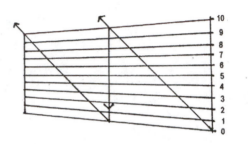

Student drawing by Tim Terry, ink on tracing paper.

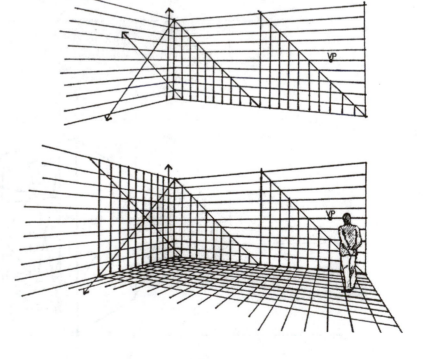

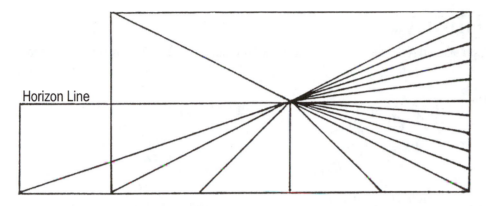

One-Point Perspective Grid

These steps explain how to create a vanishing point diagonal grid. The outside frame is used as a measuring plane in this one-point perspective grid.

(1) Each measurement of the wall plane represents 1′ intervals.
(2) Each measurement on the floor plane represents 5′ intervals.
(3) The horizon line is on the 5′ line.
(4) The vanishing point is in the center of the grid.
(5) The measurements within the grid represents 5′ x 5′ intervals. These intervals are established when the diagonal line intersects the floor lines that go to the vanishing point.

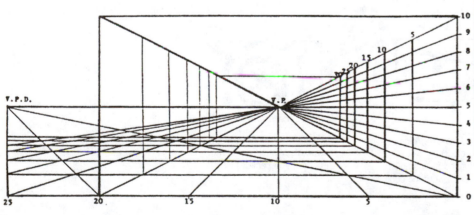

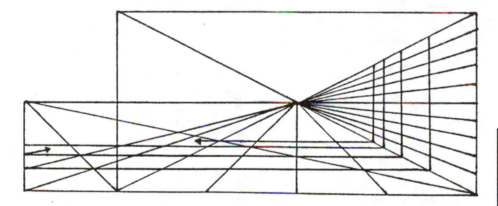

Student drawing by Tim Terry, ink on tracing paper.

Principles of Design for Visual Harmony

The following principles are an adaptation taken from the book _Design Basics_ by David A. Lauer (Holt, Rinehart and Winston, 1979). Please consider these principles when arranging your composition.

Repetition - As the term implies,something repeated in various parts of the design.

Rhythm - A design principle based on repetition, with the added element of time (interval separating points in a continuum).

a   b

Continuation - Something continues, usually a line, an edge or a direction from one form to another. Drawing (b) demonstrates the idea of continuation.

a b

Proximity - Drawing (b) makes separate elements look as if they belong together by putting these elements close together.

Symmetrical Balance - Like shapes are repeated in the same position on either side of a central vertical axis.

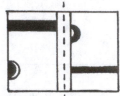

Asymmetrical Balance - Not identical on either side of a central vertical axis. A balance achieved with similar or dissimilar objects that have equal visual _weight._

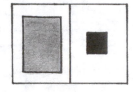

Balance by Value - Black against white is a stronger contrast than gray against white; therefore, a smaller amount of black is needed to visually balance a larger amount of gray.

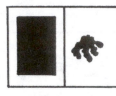

Balance by shape - The smaller form attracts the eye because of its more complicated contours. Though small, it is equally as interesting as the much larger, but duller rectangle.

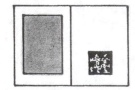

Balance by Texture - The smaller textured form holds more interest for the eye. Though small, it is equally as interesting as the larger form.

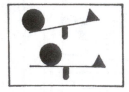

Balance by Position - A larger item placed closer to the center can be balanced by a smaller item placed out toward the edge.

Radial Balance - All elements radiate or circle out from a common central point.

Orthographic, Axonometric, and Projected Perspective Studies

Students of design must learn to express ideas graphically. Orthographic drawings (plans, elevations, and sections) are two-dimensional expressions of form. These drawings together show a measured multi-view of objects and buildings.

Axonometric drawings or paraline drawings (isometrics, plan obliques, and elevation obliques) have the ability to express volumetric forms by combining length, height, and depth as a measured graphic expression.

Projected perspectives (known as "office or common method") are drawings created from the accurate dimensions of plans and elevations. In a projected perspective drawing, lines merge toward two vanishing points on the horizon line. Perspective drawings give the observer the illusion of seeing objects and buildings in real space and time.

Goals

This exercise teaches students to express ideas graphically and challenges students to arrange objects in a composition based on principles of design.

Methodology

Historical residential buildings are studied and measured. The measured studies are done on 1000 H vellum. The studies will include the following: A roof plan, floor plan, four sided elevations, a plan oblique or isometric, and a projected perspective.

Emphasis is placed on line weight to indicate depth.

Consideration is given to the placement of each drawing in order to create a pleasing composition.

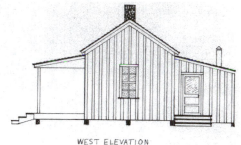

WEST ELEVATION

EAST ELEVATION

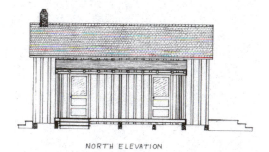

NORTH ELEVATION

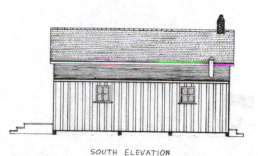

SOUTH ELEVATION

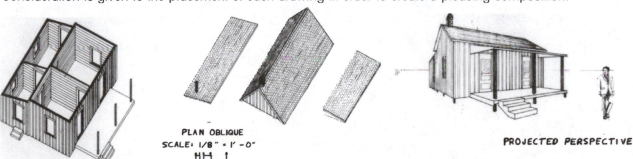

PLAN OBLIQUE
SCALE: 1/8" = 1'-0"

PROJECTED PERSPECTIVE

Student drawing by Charles Elliot, ink on 20" x 30" vellum.

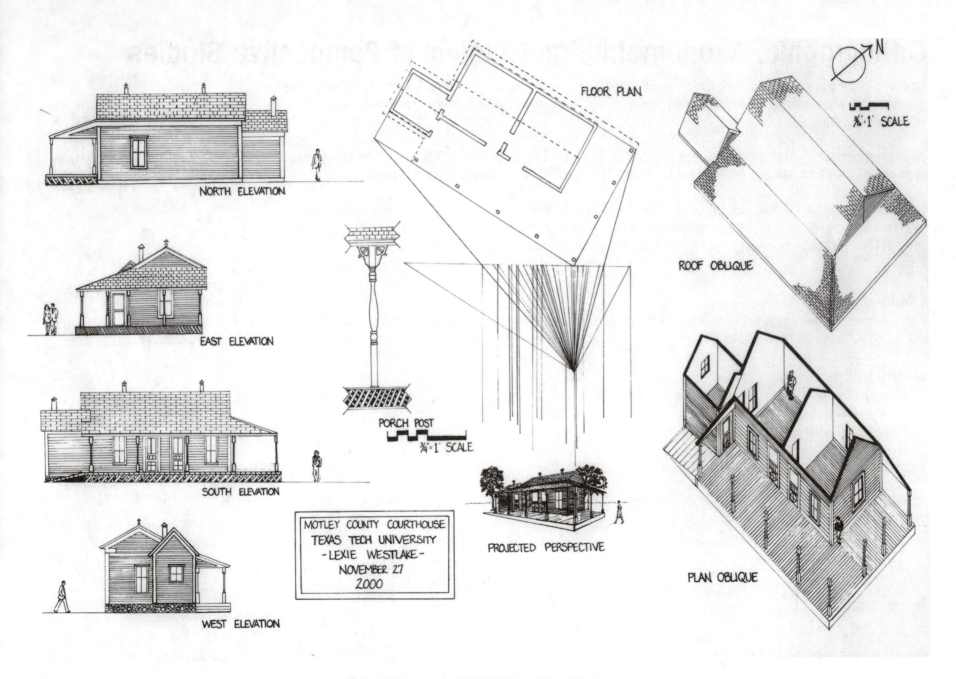

NORTH ELEVATION

EAST ELEVATION

SOUTH ELEVATION

WEST ELEVATION

FLOOR PLAN

PORCH POST

¾" = 1' SCALE

PROJECTED PERSPECTIVE

N

⅜" = 1' SCALE

ROOF OBLIQUE

PLAN OBLIQUE

MOTLEY COUNTY COURTHOUSE
TEXAS TECH UNIVERSITY
- LEXIE WESTLAKE -
NOVEMBER 27
2000

Student drawing by Lexie Westlake, ink on 20" x 30" vellum.

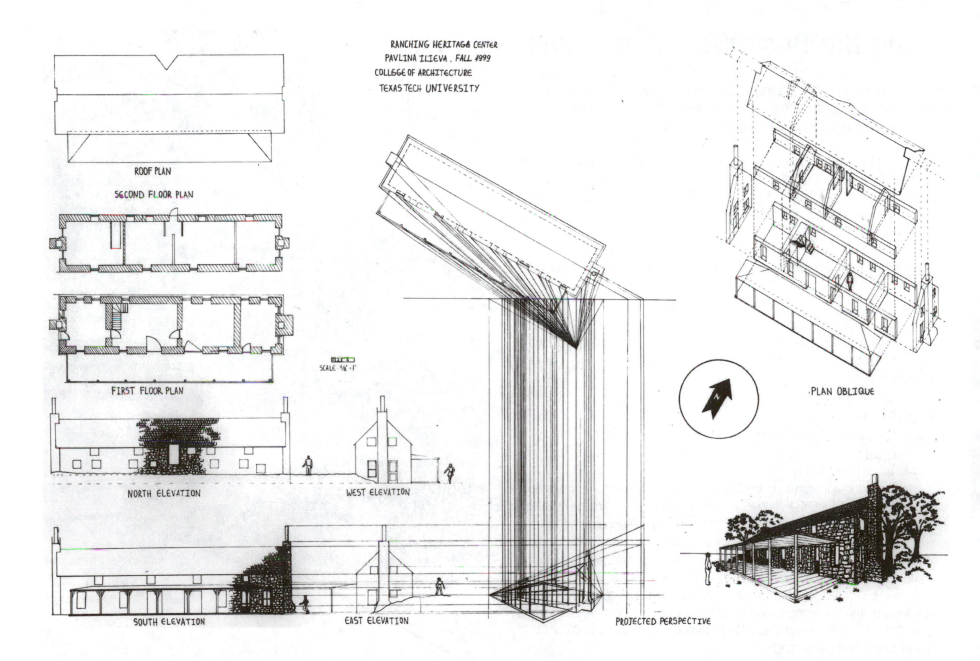

RANCHING HERITAGE CENTER
PAVLINA ILIEVA . FALL 1999
COLLEGE OF ARCHITECTURE
TEXAS TECH UNIVERSITY

ROOF PLAN

SECOND FLOOR PLAN

FIRST FLOOR PLAN

SCALE : 1/8" = 1'

NORTH ELEVATION

WEST ELEVATION

SOUTH ELEVATION

EAST ELEVATION

PROJECTED PERSPECTIVE

PLAN OBLIQUE

Student drawing by Pavlina Ilieva, ink on 20" x 30" vellum.

Using the Back Wall as a Measuring Plane

By creating a wall grid we introduce a fast, uncomplicated yet accurate method of drawing a challenging interior perspective. To form the grid, all lines are tapered equally above and below the horizon line. These lines are merging toward a second vanishing point off the paper.

To establish the width of the space, draw a line at a 45° angle down from 10′ to the floor line. Take a vertical line up from where the diagonal line touches the floor line. This will give you 10′ intervals. Wherever a diagonal line crosses a horizontal line bring a vertical line up to create 1′ intervals.

The height of furniture and other objects in the space can be measured from the back wall.

Goals

The goal of this exercise is to make complicated spaces easier to draw by using a measuring wall grid and to build confidence in the use of black and white media.

Methodology

On site drawing of an interior space. The space is chosen because of its visual interest and complexity.

Use the scaled measurements off the back wall to determine the visible vanishing point. Place the visible vanishing point on the horizon line between 5′ and 10′ feet from the edge of the drawing. The visible vanishing point represents the point directly in front of you as you stand observing the interior space. In this case all adult figures will be placed eye level to the horizon line. The width and height of all objects in this space can be determined by its relationship to the back wall. Arrange three circles, (7″ diameters) within the composition. All studies are done in black and white media (ink, graphite, wash and gray marker). Each circle is drawn in a different black and white media.

Student drawing by Kristi Davis, graphite and ink on 20″ x 30″ cold press illustration board, detail. ink

graphite

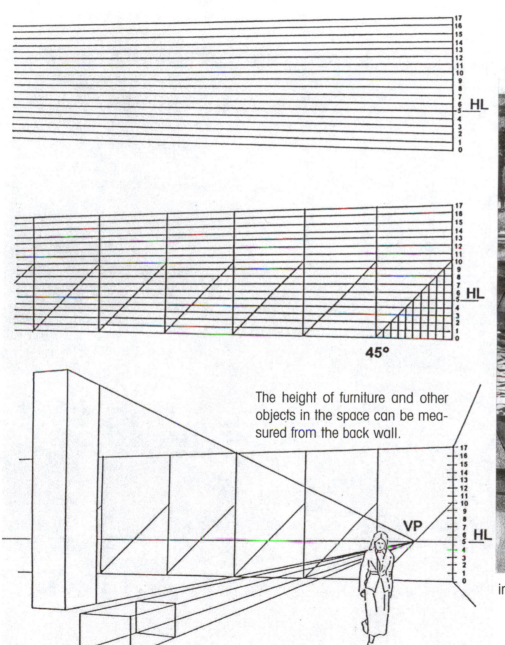

17
16
15
14
13
12
11
10
9
8
7
6
5
HL
4
3
2
1
0

17
16
15
14
13
12
11
10
9
8
7
6
5
HL
4
3
2
1
0

45°

The height of furniture and other objects in the space can be measured from the back wall.

17
16
15
14
13
12
11
10
9
8
7
VP
6
5
HL
4
3
2
1

graphite

ink wash

Student drawing by Kristi Davis, graphite and ink wash on 20 "x 30" cold press illustration board, detail.

Student drawing by Kristi Davis, graphite, ink, wash and gray marker on 20" x 30" cold press illustration board.

Student drawing by Phillip Anderson, graphite, ink, wash and gray marker on 20" x 30" cold press illustration board.

67

Spatial Collage

Jean Paul Sartre, in <u>Imagination,</u> states, "It is one thing… to apprehend directly an image and another thing to shape ideas regarding the nature of images in general." As future designers of our external world of objects, students must learn to document, record and cultivate images of our imagination. For centuries, the exploration and exploitation of one's own imagination has been the catalyst for countless possibilities and discoveries. It is through the act of drawing that one can discern or create such possibilities.

Goals

As with any drawing, students undergo an externalization of an internal process. A process of meditation takes place while focusing on the creation of planar depth and a spatially enhanced imaginary environment. In addition to recording existing mental images, students develop an understanding of a visually stimulating composition that includes the use of various drawing techniques and their relationship to other media types.

Methodology

Instructions are: While calling on previously learned design principles, compose on a 15″ x 15″ illustration board (or on the watercolor block) a collage of various architectural and non-architectural elements. Students are shown examples of various mental exercises by distinguished artists. Thereafter, they combine a variety of media, including magazine clip outs, computer generated images, photocopies, etc. and architectural drawings, an assemblage of ideas onto an infinitely deep yet perfectly flat two-dimensional space. Students are encouraged to accompany their collages with a real or fictional narrative. Often times students graphically recall a past experience or a dream. Through this process they establish motivation, inspiration and a replenishment of themselves. Group critiques often make for an interesting discussions.

Student drawings by Kimberly Gilkerson and Sylvia Guevara, mixed media on 15″ x 15″ watercolor paper.

Post Card Design

Architectural presentations reinforce, expand, and delineate architectural concepts and strategies. The postcard assignment challenges students to celebrate an architect's building or projects through comprehensive design methodologies. Existing works are used to add a research component to the exercise, to familiarize students with architectural drawings and images and to give students the opportunity to abstract concepts and ideas from design.

Goals

Students develop skills in composition by combining multiple elements into a unified presentation, selection of appropriate color-scheme and by attracting and sustaining the eye. They also learn reproductive techniques such as: scaling drawings, color assignment and inversion, layering and overlapping of images. These techniques are achieved by using various software programs and/or photocopy machines. These techniques are used in combination with hand rendered elements employing a variety of opaque, translucent, transparent colored media, such as watercolor, colored pencil, ink and markers.

Methodology

Students research and collect hardcopies of plans, sections, elevations and 3-D images (photographs, perspectives, etc.) of an architectural project under 5,000 s. f. Documentation of resources must be included with final presentation. Students are instructed to use concepts, ideas and strategies present in the existing architecture as a basis for a postcard design that "Sells!" the project. Several mock ups are required prior to final design approval. Once completed, the 25" x 40" original, which is used for class presentation and critique is reduced to a 5" x 8" postcard.

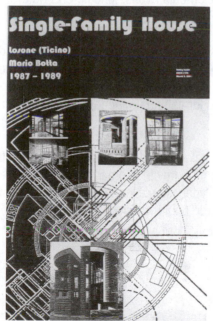 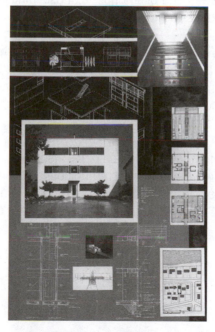 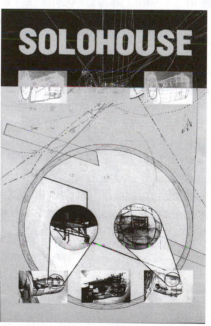

Student Postcard Designs by Bobby Lajoie, Cera M. Hammond and Jeff Floyd, originals 25" x 40" mixed media in full color.

A Board Presentation

A typical final project for the first semester drawing class is a single architectural board presentation, containing several drawings. This experience prepares students for the expectations of sophomore design class.

Goals

The primary purpose of this design problem is to afford a vehicle for developing a variety of drawing and presentation skills. Essential goals are to increase skills of organization of a comprehensive design presentation and to advance skills of effective visual communication.

Methodology

Students compose an arrangement of plans, elevations, section and paraline drawings, details and perspective drawings along with captions and a title block design. The final presentation demonstrates knowledge of architectural drawing convention, application of appropriate line quality and use of tone.

The site is 30 by 30 feet. Topography is essentially a flat plane. Within the site is a 20 by 20 feet space designated as transition area. It is located between indoor and outdoor, built form and nature, and various levels and spaces. Within the transition area, there is a 10 by 10 feet footprint of the built form. This is enclosed as a private space. You may excavate up to five feet deep for additional interior space. The built form may not exceed 20 feet above ground level. Additional interior area may be developed with changes in levels and overhangs. Landscaping includes water elements, walls, fences, and natural material such as trees, hedges, bedding plants, ground cover, lawn area and rocks.

"Magic material" makes the structure. All walls are six inches thick. The challenge is to design a memorable sense of place within the parameters listed above. Function remains limited. This is an abstract concept. There is no real or specified time or place for this problem; it is an architectonic form with interior space that provides shelter. Complicated multiple functions and mechanical systems are of little concern. This is a place to retreat from the world in order to meditate, write, study and engage in creative activity. You may develop your own scenario for purpose, but keep furnishings minimal and the design pristine and direct. The exterior form should be geometric. **Keep it simple**.

Required drawings are: a site plan showing roof, elevations, sections, floor plans, isometric, plan oblique, interior and exterior perspectives, freehand sketches, entourage elements and any additional drawings that may aid in communicating final design solution. All drawings are in black and white media. Additional requirements are a design stage model, title block, hand-lettered labels, notes and a separately typed single page design statement. Final presentation of design solution is on one sheet of vellum 24" x 36". Composition of the board is a primary factor in final evaluation. Accuracy, neatness and consistency in drawing are imperative.

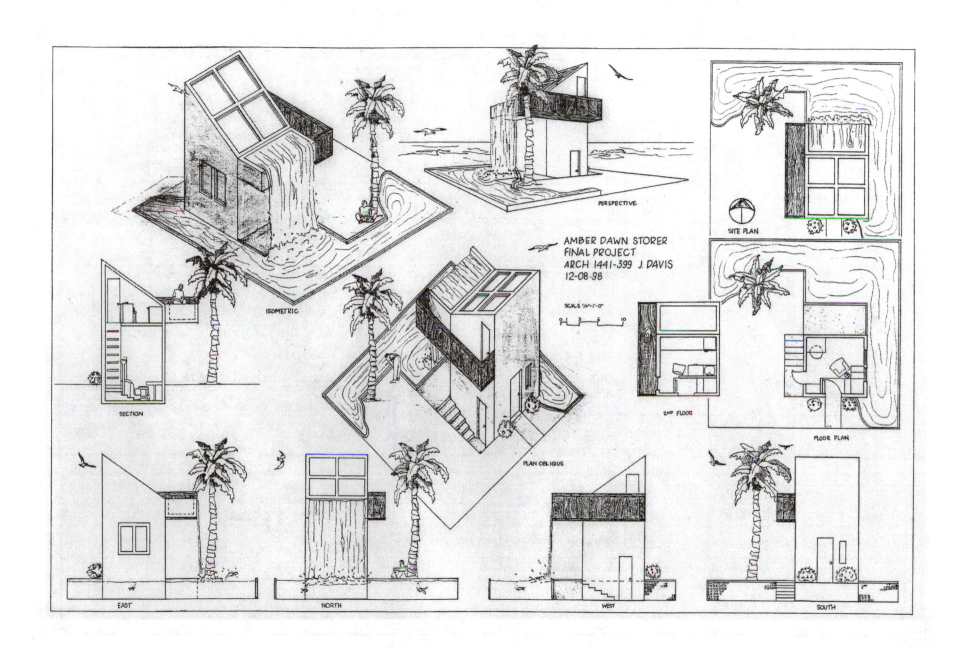

AMBER DAWN STORER
FINAL PROJECT
ARCH 1441-399 J. DAVIS
12-08-98

SCALE 1/4"=1'-0"

PERSPECTIVE

SITE PLAN

ISOMETRIC

SECTION

PLAN OBLIQUE

2ND FLOOR

FLOOR PLAN

EAST

NORTH

WEST

SOUTH

Student board presentation by Amber Dawn Storer, ink on vellum.

71

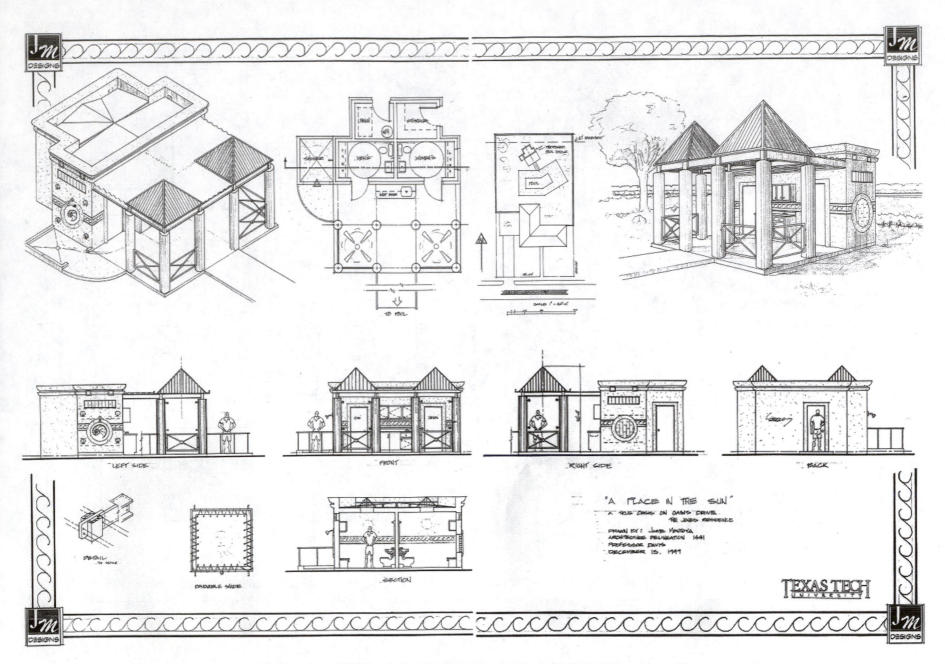

Student board presentation for a final project "Design for a Pool House" by Jaime Montoya, ink on vellum.

Learning to Paint

At this stage of development emphasis on watercolor painting acts as a vehicle to teach basic principles of color and composition. It advances the quest of learning to see. Working with paint and brush develops additional eye, mind and hand skills, which transfer well to a variety of other media in future applications. Mixing paint is a direct approach to the teaching of color theory. The use of glazes in watercolor is based on the same principles as those of colored markers, wax based pencils or any other media choice. Principles learned from these experiences easily translate to a variety of presentation applications including computer-generated renderings. Following this course, a number of students continue to produce outstanding watercolor renderings even into final thesis projects. Afterward, some render professionally as delineators and others as architects.

Watercolor painting by Richard Ferrier FAIA, architect.

Student watercolor illustration by James Britt based on photo by George Tice.

73

Color Mixing Enlarges the Color Palette

The medium of watercolor challenges the student to create bright, clear, and fluid hues. As watercolor painting skills develop, the young designer finds it easier to satisfactorily choose and apply color schemes to projects without guessing. Painting over a band of India ink shows the levels of transparency or opacity of each color. The creation of a color wheel helps in sorting through the many possibilities when choosing color schemes.

Goals

The goals are to increase the range of color possibilities and to identify the various levels of transparency.

Methodology

Color mixing is accomplished in seven steps. A line of seven, (one-inch) squares is created. On either end of the seven squares, paint examples of the two tubes of paint being mixed. The middle-square shows the two colors mixed with equal parts. On either end the colors are mixed in a combination of four parts to one part, then three parts to two parts (as shown in the illustration). Each color from the tube of paint is painted over a band of India ink to observe levels of transparency or opacity.

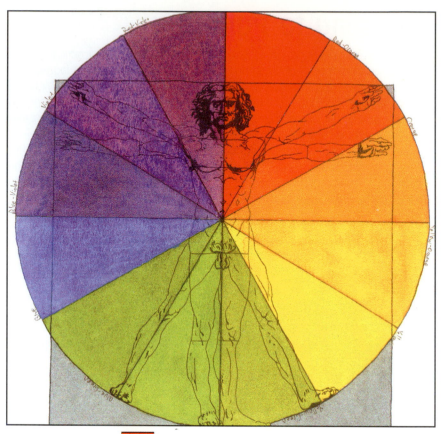

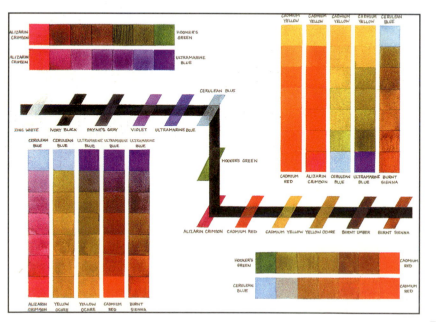

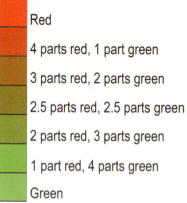

- Red
- 4 parts red, 1 part green
- 3 parts red, 2 parts green
- 2.5 parts red, 2.5 parts green
- 2 parts red, 3 parts green
- 1 part red, 4 parts green
- Green

Student work by Jasmin Silvas, watercolor and ink on 15" x 20" watercolor paper.

74

Skies

In architectural presentations, skies assist in the definition of the built structure. A good solution for a light valued building is to use a dark sky to silhouette it. Conversely, to define a dark building one keeps darker parts of the sky high and away from the structure. A soft atmospheric sky is used to contrast a rigid built form. Sky painting can also add movement and rhythm to an otherwise static composition. The painting of a series of imaginary and observed skies provides experimentation with wet into wet techniques and the use of unexpected non-local color.

Goals

Students strive to "see" and then create atmosphere and drama in sky compositions. In addition, these little paintings free the student to express feelings and emotions. Some projects subtly transform into a type of abstract expressionism.

Methodology

Instructions are: Experiment with painting a variety of skies wet into wet. Utilize transparent and opaque watercolor techniques. A sky may actually be nothing more than a graded wash. Pre-wet the entire formatted area and splash on a blue sky wash and let it run. Keep tilting the board to control the graduation. Apply and lift paint with a sponge or large brush. Experiment with a variety of color combinations and techniques. Work rapidly and intuitively. Attempt to delineate a sky on a clear day, with a storm front rolling in, at sunset, with puffy white clouds or in a West Texas dust storm. Notice that skies appear to get lighter as they approach the horizon.

Student sky paintings by Jeremy Todd, Ryan Bemberg, Naomi Clark, Robert Peterson, and Emily Morris, watercolor on 8" x 10" watercolor paper.

Isometric Shade and Shadow

Color Studies with Watercolor

This is a vehicle used to explore a variety of techniques and to develop skill in application of color with a paintbrush. It provides an opportunity to teach shade and paraline shadow construction as well as basic color theory.

Goals

Students review and expand skills with paraline drawing and mechanical paraline shade and shadow casting. Simple color theories through specific color schemes are explored. Students construct simple orthogonal architectonic compositions, cast shadows and develop specific color schemes. Application of a variety of transparent watercolor techniques is presented. Titles give practice in hand lettering technique.

Methodology

Instructions are: Start with basic isometric cube and design increasingly complex architectonic forms within a small format. Divide a standard 15" x 20" watercolor block into four equal sections with a ¼" to ½" masking tape border to get an appropriate size format. Use a horizontal bearing and an angle of altitude of 45 degrees to shade and cast shadows. Paint the cube in a monochromatic color scheme in a "French Graded Wash" technique, sequentially layering each value without changing color. Draw a second design comprised of two basic rectilinear units. Construct shadows and paint the composition in an analogous color scheme. Include three or more different blocks in the third composition and paint with a complementary color scheme. Include curved forms, slants or overhangs to increase complexity and paint a fourth in a triadic color scheme. Continue to develop forms that are more complex with additional color schemes. Use masking techniques on some and paint wet on dry in layers without masking on others. A variation of this assignment is to use marker and colored pencils as the media.

Student color studies by Jeff Rogus, Jason Darling, Eric Pate, Bryce Hamels, Danny Beluska, and Robert Peterson, watercolor on 8" x 10" watercolor paper

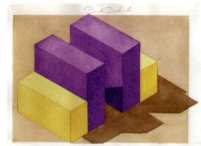
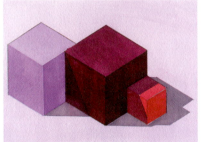

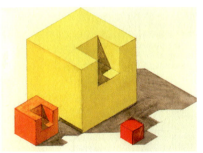

Skies Meet Built Form

The natural extension of the sky painting project leads directly into imposition of built form on various skies. In a rendering skies frame and accent the architecture as well as contribute life and movement.

Goals

Students develop organizational and rendering skills by creating appropriate skies to complement specific architectural structures.

Methodology

Students develop their compositions from photographic references of built forms that they find interesting. Compositions are cropped to emphasize the juncture and relationship between the hard-edged built form and the atmospheric sky. Color and value relationships are analyzed.

Student paintings by Paula Yeager, Eric Pate, Tayna Nash, and Heather Burt, watercolor on 8" x 10" watercolor paper.

77

Fruit

A fun project for class or homework is "the Great Fruit Contest." This is a competition to see who can use their painting skill to create the most desirable fruit or vegetable. Judging is by popular vote or by invited jury.

Goals

The Great Fruit Contest increases student awareness of the importance of visual communication skills. Further, it develops visual sensitivity to the environment, problem solving ability and general painting and drawing skills.

Methodology

Prior to beginning work, students are shown various examples of watercolor still life painting. A quick demonstration is instructional and motivational for most students. This class project requires each student to bring a fruit or vegetable to class. If it is a homework assignment, they are told simply to paint the most appetizing fruit or vegetable possible.

Student "Fruit Competition" entries by Danny Beluska, Paula Yeager, Michael Zimmerman, Chris Mazza, Able Hernandez, Heather Burt, various sizes, watercolor on watercolor paper.

Signs

A set of antonyms is used for a lettering and design project. These words represent materials or conditions (physical or emotional). This project is a continued study of media application and color theory. The object is to make appropriate decisions with principles of design and color choices to graphically communicate to an observer the meaning of the words. The design of the letters becomes an illustration.

Goals

Students expand their creative expression by combining and contrasting visual, verbal and emotional concepts in a single visual statement.

Methodology

Instructions are: Choose a set of terms from the list below or propose your alternative suggestions to the instructor for approval. Research type styles, textures and patterns as well as information on physical, emotional and psychological implication of color choices for your design decisions. Fill the space with a composition from the letters of the words illustrated. The media is principally watercolor on paper, however, exploration of mixed media is encouraged. Develop a single plate from half of a sheet (10" x 15") from the watercolor block, which may later be divided into two separate sheets. Borders are used to accent and define the space.

Suggestions: hot/cold, cat/dog, old/young, soft/hard, sun/rain, wet/dry, slow/fast, smooth/rough, sharp/dull, open/closed, up/down, fire/ice, happy/sad, calm/nervous, sleep/awake, work/play, brick/glass, steel/stone, wood/leather, mad/glad, hurt/help, rich/poor, strong/weak, alive/dead, fur/feather, land/water, empty/full.

Student projects, sets of antonyms illustrated by Andy Nastoupil, Paula Yeager, Corey Cash, Robert Peterson and Darrellee Clem, mixed media.

Poster Design

Designing a poster involves the harmonious placement of multiple parts. This is a necessary requirement of any design effort. A vocabulary of design principles must be used to achieve visual harmony. (Please refer to the design principles on page 60).

Goals

The goal of this project is to introduce the vocabulary of design principles to be used in presentation drawings that involves multiple parts in the composition.

Methodology

On a sheet of 20" x 30" 1000 H velum, design a poster using an architectural subject. Considerable research should be given to the information used to compose the design. The objective is to express the essence of the subject matter in the poster design. After the design is finished make a diazo print, (blue line, black line or brown line). Apply color to the diazo print using one or more color scheme. The final presentation is done in watercolor, color pencil, color marker or a combination of media.

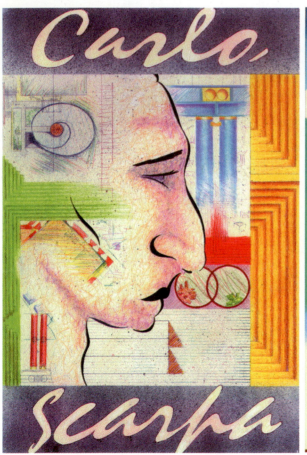 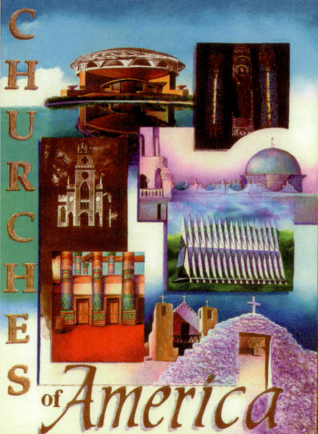 

Student poster designs by Dominique Houriel, Kristy Davis and Chase Parker, color pencil and mixed media on 20" x 30" diazo prints.

Fenestrations

An opening in a wall is a fenestration. A door or window, open or closed, glazed or unglazed, offers students opportunities to study a variety of architectural details. By focusing on a fenestration, they observe at a scale that shows more detail than is typical in most presentation rendering. Just as architectural training helps one to draw buildings, drawing buildings supports architectural training. One learns to see through observation. Viewing architectural detail with the goal of drawing gives insight into construction and finish (design development).

Goals

Students develop a watercolor (or mixed media) composition that focuses on a fenestration and the surrounding detail. They gain experience in rendering building materials, illustrating shade and shadow, and developing color schemes.

Methodology

Students are asked to find interesting photographic examples of doors and windows for resources. Instructions are: Sketch lightly in pencil on formatted watercolor paper. Paint according to an identifiable color scheme, and explore the potential of the paint to communicate building materials at the appropriate scale. An alternate approach to this project is to vary the media. Good choices are colored pencils on toned paper, or mixed media such as marker and colored pencil on toned tracing paper.

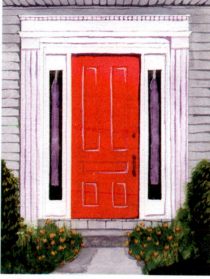

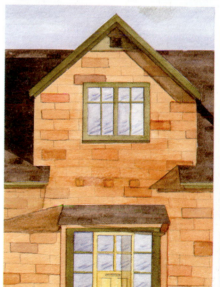

Student fenestration renderings by Jon Long, Jamie Reed, Ryan Bemberg, Paula Yeager, Marissa Brown and Linden Albers, watercolor on 8" x 10" watercolor paper.

Bird House

Architects occasionally design small-scale projects for non-human clients. Frank Lloyd Wright once designed a doghouse. A freshman architecture student at Texas Tech University won an award in a national competition for his doghouse design. Bird-houses by famous architects such as Michel Stern, Michael Graves and others have been auctioned at charity dinners. Locally, the Lubbock chapter of the AIA has sponsored a Birdhouse Competition and there is an annual Birdhouse Competition for the South Plains Food Bank.

Goals

Students develop skills in producing an architectural presentation that informs and persuades. By creating an original three-dimensional structure, they develop architectural design skills.

Methodology

This project is an early experience in presentation of an original design concept in full color. A single board includes plans, elevations, sections and three-dimensional drawings. Instructions are: Research an architect or an architectural style. Explore multiple ideas in sketch form before final presentation drawings are begun. Use tracing paper, and colored pencils for the initial idea sketches. Plan the board layout and establish an appropriate color scheme before beginning to paint.

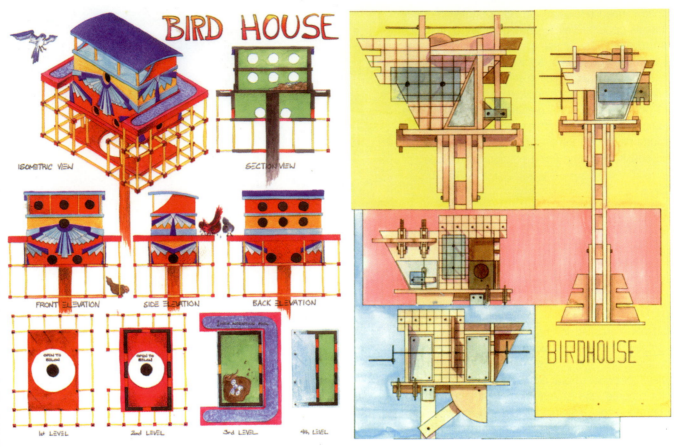

Student designs for birdhouses by Daniel Pruske, and Todd Wascher, watercolor on 15" x 20" watercolor paper.

Suggestions — *Architects*: Richard Meier, Frank Gehry, Le Corbusier, Louis Kahn, Michael Graves, Buckminster Fuller, Philip Johnson, Julia Morgan, Rennie Mackintosh, Robert Venturi, and Charles Moore.
Architectural Styles: Classical, Neo-Classical, Modern, Post Modern, Deconstructivism, De Stijl and the Arts and Crafts Movement.

Texturing Techniques and Architectural Details

Texture plays a major role in visual communication. Texture becomes a factor in communicating visual depth. Many surfaces from a distance appear to be smooth, whereas, the closer we get, the more uneven and varied the surface becomes. There are many techniques available for expressing the tactile quality of objects.

Goals

The goal of this exercise is to acquire an arsenal of texturing techniques to express visual distance and visual interest. This exercise also encourages visual awareness in discerning different textures.

Methodology

Texturing techniques in both watercolor and color pencil are practiced in class. This assignment requires a perspective architectural detail that includes three or more different materials. Use as many texturing techniques as possible to create a composition that communicates depth and the surface quality of the materials.

MULTIDIRCTION   HATCHING   STIPPLING   NON-DIRECTION   LAYERING

SCRAPING   BLENDING   MASKING   BURNISHING   SGRAFFITO

Texturing techniques in color pencil

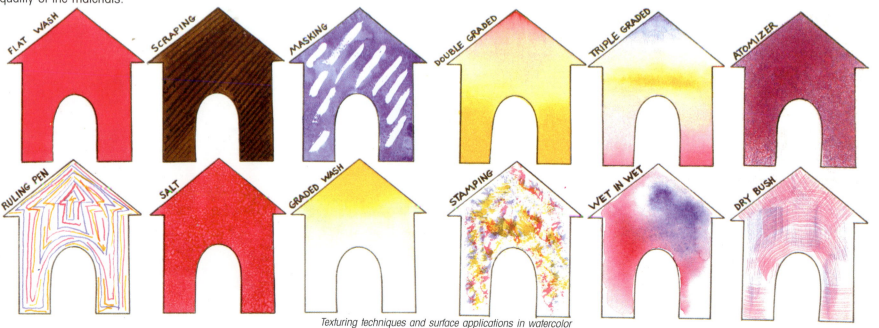

Texturing techniques and surface applications in watercolor

83

Micro Studies

Observation of objects and materials at different distances and points of view challenge perception and delineation skills. Materials drawn at different scales are rendered in different ways, with more or less detail dependent on how close the viewer is to the object. The object of this exercise is the continuing quest of learning to see.

Goals

Students become aware of how a "photo-real" painting can also be an abstract composition. They strive to match local color, emulate actual texture and master perspective drawing at a micro scale.

Methodology

Students find their own compositions by "zooming in" with their eyes on the juncture of different materials in their immediate environment. This is an exercise in accurate freehand drawing and painting. The quarter page format is a good size for this level of detail. Emphasis is placed on the abstract composition or arrangement within the space. These little gems of paintings may take from four to six hours and necessitate intense concentration.

Student "Micro Study" paintings by Brent Wright, Brandon Blount, Jamie Reed, Bryce Hamels, Able Hernandez and Allison Chambers, watercolor on 8" x 10" watercolor paper.

Oral presentations and group critiques of this project will include discussion of basic principles of composition: proportion systems, balance, rhythm, emphasis, and direction of eye movement within the composition. Students should be able to explain application of color schemes as well as technical issues such as how various textures were achieved and use of mixed media.

Student Micro Studies by Dominique Houriet and Kristi Wolking, 15" x 20' and by , Eric Pate, Fernando Gonzalez, Able Hernandez and William Bussard, 8" x 10' on watercolor paper.

Car Painting

Automobiles are standard entourage elements that every delineator must draw at one time or another. Cars give scale, activity, purpose and vitality to architectural subjects in the same manner as people and trees. Additionally, cars provide challenges to the delineator with shiny, high gloss curvilinear surfaces, transparences, and unusual problems with perspective.

Goals

Students strive to successfully render in color reflective irregular surfaces. They address the challenges inherent with foreshortening, proportion and other problems in drawing a car. One objective is to achieve a "showy" product, which builds confidence and makes a positive contribution to the portfolio.

Methodology

Students are given the option of working from commercial photographs of vehicles or from their personal photographs. The class goes to a parking lot adjacent to the classroom and sketches cars as a preliminary exercise. Composition is worked out prior to transferring to watercolor paper. Size is limited to the formatted watercolor block and is effective as small as one quarter sheet. Composite compositions are encouraged, with the car coming from one source and the environment from another. Traditional transparent watercolor is used with some gouache or mixed media.

Student car studies by Fernando Gonzalez, Jason Trego, Linden Albers, Whitney Blackwielder, Jill Pickett, Danny Beluska and Paula Yeager, various sizes 5" x 20" to 8" x 10", watercolor and mixed media.

86

Storefront Color Schemes

Color harmony, as the term implies, consist of colors, which, when placed together create a pleasant stimulation. There are four methods, which may be used, either separately or in combination to produce color harmony. One method is through the use of complementary colors; the second is by means of using colors that are closely associated to each other on the color wheel; the third is the use of one hue which varies in value from light to dark or from dark to light; the forth involves using colors that are equally spaced on the color wheel.

For this exercise we will use the following color harmonies or color schemes as they are often called:
Analogous- Three colors allied to each other due to their side by side relation on the color wheel.
Analogous with Complement- Three colors, allied to each other due to their side by side relationship on the color wheel, with the addition of the color diametrically opposite it on the color wheel.
Complementary- Colors that are diametrically opposite each other on the color wheel. When these colors are placed side by side, each makes the other appear to be more intense.
Split Complementary- A split complementary is made up of three colors; one complementary and the two colors on either side of the opposite complementary color.
Monochromatic- The use of one color. In this color scheme the color may vary in value and chroma from light to dark or from dark to light.
Monochromatic with Complement- The variation of one color from light to dark or from dark to light with it's complementary color.
Triad- Any three colors that are equidistant on a color wheel and whose connecting path form an approximate equilateral triangle.
Tetrad- Any four colors that are equidistant on a color wheel and whose connecting path form a square inside a color wheel.

Goals

This exercise introduces color harmony and creates confidence in making decisions related to color.

Methodology

Photographs are taken of local storefront shopping centers, which are used by the students as a point of departure for creating their own storefront shopping centers drawn in elevation. The complete assignment, consist of eight storefront elevations painted in watercolor with each storefront having a different color scheme, with entourage and shade and shadow. Color unity may be achieved by using tonality. Tonality refers to the dominance of a single color that would be common in each color scheme.

Student drawings by Sze-Lyn Lim, Kayla Eady and Jasmin Silvas, top to bottom, ink and watercolor on 15" x 20" watercolor paper.

Elevations

A quick way to visualize architectural color and design is by elevation studies.

Goals

Students are able to quickly produce professional looking color elevations.

Methodology

Diazo prints of elevation drawings at scale are provided for students to trace onto watercolor paper by means of a light box. Time is not spent designing original buildings since this is a color study exercise and is intended to explore media and rendering techniques. For some of the examples shown, blue prints of HABS studies were given to students. Studies explored painting with transparent watercolor on 30 pound watercolor paper. An extension of this project uses marker and colored pencil on tracing paper with the same subject and at the same scale.

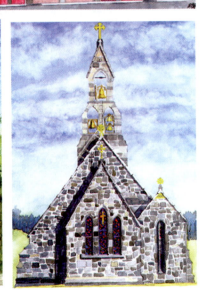

Student elevation studies by Cory Cash, John Driscoll, Stewart Boddee, Fernando Gonzalez, Kyle Brown and Bill Carroll, watercolor on 15" x 20" watercolor paper.

Interior Color Scheme

Considerable research has been done on the physiological and psychological responses to color. Placid colors have a calming effect. Bright vibrant colors can raise the blood rate. Cool colors in an interior space can evoke a feeling of cool temperatures. Warm colors can evoke a feeling of warm temperatures. Because of our strong response to color, it is important to have confidence and sensitivity when making decisions concerning color harmony.

Goals

This exercise re-enforces ideas about color harmony and decision-making concerning color possibilities.

Methodology

On a sheet of 20" x 30" cold press illustration board draw an interior perspective from a photograph in a magazine. The photograph should be no smaller than 5" x 6" so that all objects may be seen clearly. The drawing should be divided into three equal parts. Each divided part should depict a different color scheme. The drawing should be completed in watercolor, color pencil, color marker or a combination of media.

Student drawings by Tim Terry, left, and Julie Stelz, right, using color pencil and color marker on 20" x 30" cold press illustration board.

Tiny Houses

This full color architectural board presentation is based on an existing small-scale project in order to avoid a lengthy design phase.

Goals

Students develop skills in the selection of appropriate color schemes, organization of multiple drawings on a single board, and application of hand lettering. They develop an appreciation of drama and eye appeal in a finished presentation. Fluency and speed in implementation of a design presentation project is improved.

Methodology

Project handouts are distributed. Students choose an existing design for their subject. Resources provide a scaled plan and elevation drawings. Complete documentation for the original designer and source must be included in the text on the final presentation. Students are given a choice of media for presentation. Instructions are: Use an organizational grid for planning the layout. Avoid hard static symmetry, this is an informal presentation. Attempt more dramatic "stage set" layouts. Draw as large as possible without overcrowding. Use texts such as Architectural Graphics by Francis D. K. Ching to research architectural drawing convention, hierarchy of line weight, and organizational ideas before drawing on the final board. Employ thumbnail planning sketches to explore a variety of options before committing paint to board. Required drawings for this presentation are: site plan with north arrow and graphic scale; section; elevation views; paraline drawing and perspective that includes appropriate entourage; and a construction detail. Establish an identifiable color scheme. Design a title block that includes name of the project, your name, date/course information, and text explaining or describing the project. All lettering should be done by hand.

The book, Tiny Houses by Larry Walker, was used as a resource for this project.

Student board presentation by Ruel Mendoza, marker and colored pencil on 11" x 17" toned tracing paper.

Placing an Architectural Sculptural Unit into a Built Environment

The ability to convincingly place objects and buildings in an environment is a very important skill. Consideration must be given to scale, multiple vanishing points, entourage and the consistency of light, which create shade and shadow.

Goals

This exercise offers an opportunity to investigate presentation techniques in orthographic drawing, axonometric drawing, and perspective drawing.

Methodology

An architectonic sculpture is created from the subtracted parts of a solid unit which measures 10′ wide, 6′ deep, and 18′ tall. This sculpture should be designed at ¼″ scale in plan, elevation, isometric and plan oblique. A model should be built at a ½″ scale. The model is used for studies in mechanical shade and shadow. A projected perspective is enlarged and placed in an environment. Many studies are done on tracing paper before committing to the final presentation. The final presentation is done in watercolor, color pencil, color marker or a combination of media.

Student drawing by Sze-Lyn Lim, watercolor and ink on 15″ x 20″ watercolor paper.

Student drawing by Jeff Palmer, watercolor and ink on 15″x 20″ watercolor paper.

Two-Point and One-Point Perspective Gallery Presentations

By using a two and one-point perspective grid, it is possible to create complex interior perspectives with assurance and confidence. The grid enables you to make accurate measurements in interior perspectives. (Please refer to the two-point and one-point perspective grids on pages 58 and 59).

Goals

The goal of this exercise is to re-enforce skills in making presentation drawings.

Methodology

On a sheet of 30" x 40" cold press illustration board, design **two interiors** for an art gallery. In the two exhibition spaces there are five figurative paintings and three figurative sculptures. There are four or more people observing the art exhibition in each interior space.

On one wall there is a large window with a recognizable view of your campus. In the ceiling there is a sky light, which you are to design. Each interior space has a different color scheme. The dimensions of the rooms are 20' wide, 30' deep and 10' high. There is a 2' x 2' furred down on either side of the ceiling, which houses the heating and cooling ducts. These specifications are used only as a point of departure; variations are encouraged and expected.

One interior space shows a one-point perspective view and the other shows a two-point perspective view. Many studies are done on tracing paper before committing to the final presentation. The most successful drawings are transferred to cold press illustration board using graphite paper. The final presentations are done in watercolor, color pencil, color marker or a combination of media. The horizon line is at 5'. Adult figures should be placed eye level to the horizon line. Shadows should be created from a dominant light source, which comes from the center of the room.

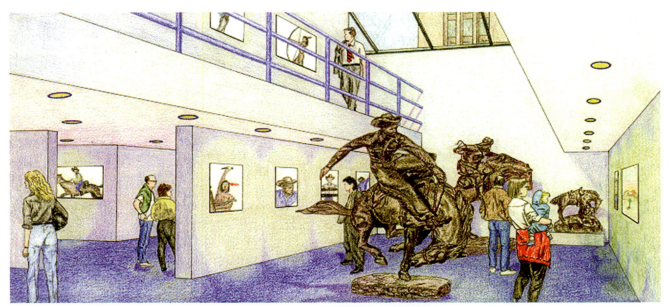

Student drawing by Brian West, colored pencil on 14" x 24" cold press illustration board.

Triptych Board Presentation

A final project requires an extended period of time. Two typical exercises are described — Storage Shed, and Belveder at the End of the Pier. Concepts are the same for both. These projects are presented as brief architectural programs.

Storage Shed

Program: Your client wants a small multi-purpose building for his back yard. Your job is to develop potential design solutions with the aid of the client. The site is the southeast corner of a flat grassy back yard in Lubbock, TX. A wooden fence five feet high marks the perimeter of the yard with a flowerbed five feet wide parallel to the fence. The principal view of the proposed structure in the back yard is from the northwest corner. Primary activities associated with this building are re-potting houseplants and storing garden supplies, tools, outdoor furniture, seasonal decorations and several large oil paintings. Daylighting, insulation and ventilation are required. The client appreciates innovative architecture inspired by oriental vernacular. Spatial requirements depend on the client being able to perform outlined activities, yet limiting overall dimensions as much as possible. For inspiration reference Japanese teahouses, the work of Frank Lloyd Wright and Faye Jones. Presentation requirements are three boards (11" x 17" each), drawings produced at an architectural scale, graphic scale and north arrow, a title block and notes hand lettered. Drawings required are a site plan showing context; floor plan; exterior perspective with entourage; exterior elevations; a section and a construction detail. Write a design essay describing the three most important concepts of your design solution.

Storage Shed board presentations by Matt Roy and Michael Bryan, watercolor on three 11" x 17" boards.

Belveder* at the End of the Pier

Program: Your clients own a two-acre lake surrounded by wooded rolling hills in south Mississippi. They are retired. Both have knowledge of architecture and an appreciation of whimsy. Their home is located a short distance from the lake through a wooded area. The lake site is a pristine, isolated place where one can commune with nature. The environment is romantic. Water-plants float and weave profusely in the shallows adjacent to the bank. Black willows and other water loving trees randomly encroach the lake. The clients want a structure where one may relax over the water and immerse the senses in the sights, smells and sounds of nature. Like a gazebo**, the structure you are commissioned to design provides pleasant views, shelter from the harsh sun. Additionally, it protects from annoying insects. It is handicapped accessible, safe for small children and secure from vandals when not in use. Presentation requirements are three 11" x 17" boards, drawings produced at an architectural scale, graphic scale and north arrow, human figure(s), title block and notes hand lettered. Communication of your design is the core of this project. Include a written design statement.

*Belveder — A building or architectural feature of a building, designed and situated to look out on a pleasing scene.
**Gazebo — A freestanding roofed structure, usually open on the sides, affording shade and rest.

Belveder board presentations by Ruel Mendoza and Beverly Norris, watercolor on three 11" x 17" boards.

94

Portfolio

The following portfolio by professional artists/architects directly represents the drawing program in the College of Architecture at Texas Tech University. Our program translates its meaning by way of works from our former students, firms that hire our graduates and faculty who support it.

Paul Stevenson Oles, FAIA. Boston Federal Courthouse, Henry N. Cobb, FAIA, architect, Pei, Cobb, Freed & Partners, wax based pencil on photographic print "retrocolor" 15″ x 8½″.

Richard Ferrier FAIA, architect, "Windows & Fragments = Memory and Desire", watercolor, photoimages, metals, graphite on 22" x 30" watercolor paper, 1994.

96

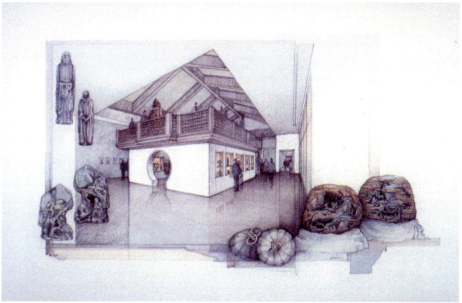

Richard Ferrier FAIA, architect, Hsieh Island stamps, watercolor; Tower illustration, architectural studio demo, watercolor; CROW Museum, watercolor drawings; Jefferson, memorial WDC, watercolor; Proposed Dallas Tower: Kohn Pederson Fox, Architects, graphite & watercolor; Bank Tower Lobby: Cesar Pelli, Architect, graphite & watercolor, various sizes.

David Farrell, architect, Good Fulton & Farrell Architects, Dallas, Texas, watercolor on 22" x 30" watercolor paper.

James T. Davis MFA, artist/educator, "Details", watercolor on 8" x 10" watercolor paper; illustrations for the Buddy Holly Museum, Lubbock, TX, mixed media on 11" x 17" board; Merket Center, Texas Tech, graphite and watercolor 15" x 20" watercolor paper; Courtyard of the Merket Center, graphite and watercolor on 15" x 20" watercolor paper.

David Farrell, architect, Good Fulton & Farrell Architects, Dallas, Texas, watercolor on 21" x 16" trash paper.

Robbie Fusch, architect, Fusch - Serold & Partners, Dallas, Texas, Gate House For Residential Development, watercolor on 11" x 17" medium weight bond print.

Ben Shacklette, architect/illustrator, Proposed Medical Facility, Mescalero, New Mexico, watercolor; Jonathan Rogers Waste Water Treatment Facility, El Paso, Texas, Smith & Cooper, Architects-Engineers, watercolor.

Ben Shacklette, architect/illustrator, elevation studies Proposed Residential Treatment Center, Lubbock County, B. Shacklette/SLS Partnership, pencil, ink & marker.

Phil Hamilton, illustrator, Looney Ricks Kiss Architects, Memphis, Tennessee, Project for a Hotel in San Juan, Puerto Rico, ink and marker on 11" x 17" drawing paper.

Bin Yu, architect, Dermarest & Associates, Dallas, Texas, OSU Suites, pen and marker on 11" x 17" trash paper.

Bin Yu, architect, Demarest & Associates, Dallas, Texas, OSU Apartments, pen and marker on 11" x 17" trash paper.

Two illustrations of towers by Texas Tech graduates: Paul Stevenson Oles, FAIA, artist, architect, author and perhaps the premier architectural perspectivist in the world; and Richard Ferrier, FAIA, artist, architect, educator, and probably the best watercolorist in Texas. Both these delineations are in the tradition of Hugh Ferriss, the father of American architectural illustration. In each image, ominous dark skies serve as backdrops for imposing, asymmetrically placed towers in vertical formats.

Richard Ferrier, FAIA, drawing of the Federal Building Restoration at Fair Park, Dallas, TX, graphite on paper.

Paul Stevenson Oles, FAIA, Office Tower, Paris, France, architect Henry N. Cobb, FAIA of Pei Cobb Freed & Partners.

This drawing in black wax based pencil on 18" x 8" vellum with watercolor paper underlay, won the Hugh Ferris Memorial Prize given by the American Society of Architectural Perspectivists in 1996.

Richard Ferrier FAIA, architect, Tower House, conceptual watercolor and sketches

Texas architect/educator/illustrator, Richard Ferrier has for some years been involved in what he describes as "an ongoing investigation of architectural potential." This statement refers to his series of highly organized abstract drawings and constructions. He feels that these compositions provide us with a method of exploring the juxtapositions of architectural considerations. Integrated Images of architectural components, the landscape and windows allow a vision into and out of reality, they provoke intellectual as well as intuitive response from the viewer. Although difficult to categorize, work from his "Windows and Fragments" series have won numerous awards.

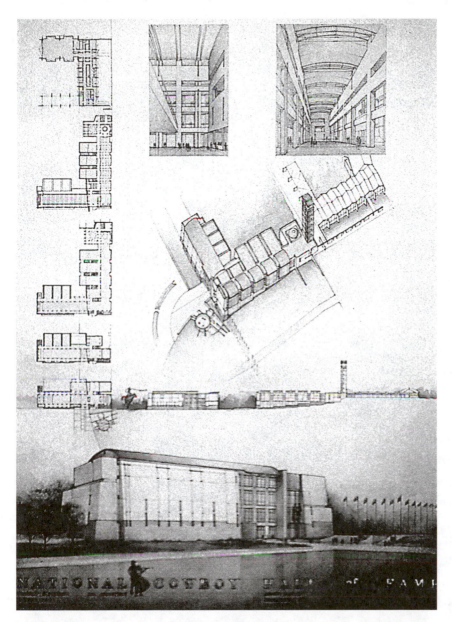

Dallas in Context: Architecture since 1945

Richard Ferrier FAIA, architect, Cowboy Hall of Fame Competition, Firm X, watercolor composite; Dallas Architectural Exhibit Catalog Cover Illustration, graphite and watercolor; Bonito @ Chaco Canyon, graphite and watercolor, various sizes.

SOUTHLAND TOWER

Architecture in a Pluralistic society

Architecture is a reflection of society and this is a most unique time:
Pluralism

multiple readings, transformations, recycling, adaptive reuse and other considerations.

For this sketch, I considered the transformation from a singular/static use .... a corporate office tower & hotel complex to a more diverse and interactive urban protagonist.

Richard Ferrier FAIA
Firm X

146 ⬚ DOWNTOWN   D MAGAZINE OCTOBER 1996

We gathered at the 8.0 one day to talk about downtown. Over cocktails and soft drinks we talked about the men who built downtown, the structures they built and rebuilt over the years, and the men and women who are fighting to rebuild and rethink downtown now. But what about the future? What might happen with those buildings that as yet have no champions? Out came the pens and cocktail napkins, and the talk grew lively. The next week we enlisted five architects to join in the fun and to sketch for us what they would do in the future—with no limitations of time or money—with those buildings whose best days right now are in the past.

Richard Ferrier FAIA, architect, Napkin Sketch, D Magazine Oct. 1996

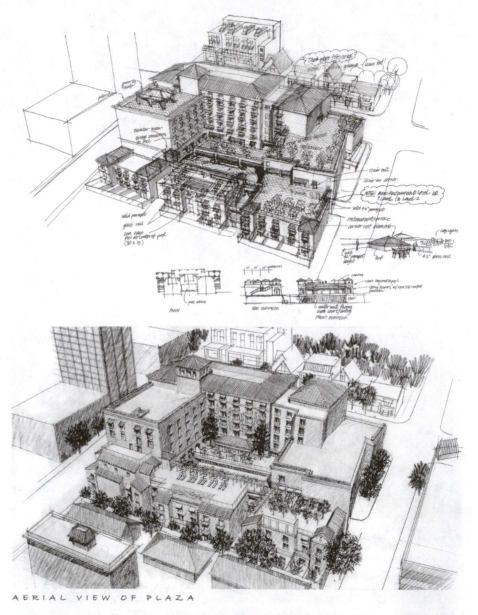

PLAN   SIDE ELEVATION   FRONT ELEVATION

AERIAL VIEW OF PLAZA

50 SUNSET BOULEVARD
st Hollywood, California

Three Architecture
17 November 1998

Carl Ede, architect, Three Architecture, Dallas, Texas, Ink and pencil on 11″ x 17″ drawing paper.

108

STREET ELEVATION

0 5 10 20 ft.

Advice for interns

1.   **On Meeting Deadlines:**

    A. Have mental toughness. Never say never, or that I can not do something.

    B. Prepare far in advance, not the night before the presentation is due.

    C. Students must realize that doing work from 12:00-6:00 a.m. in the morning does not work in an office. (I can show you many unsuccessful employees that fail with this mentality.)

2.   Acquire the ability to solve problems by thinking on your own, not just have someone redline drawings.

3.   Develop the ability to draw by hand to display an idea (sketches, details, perspectives,elevations and color presentations). Many interns talk a good game, but never produce ideas or drawings.

4.   The computer is a tool that too many interns try to use too much. Use it to your advantage, but not for everything. Remember, designing is a process of ideas, not something that a computer thinks of and spits out.

Christopher J. Kupcunas, Principal. Bryant, Burton, Kupcunas Architects

Drawings on this page by Christopher Kupcunas, Architect, Bryant, Burton, Kupcunas Architects, Dallas Texas, marker and pen and ink.

Virginia Mahaley Thompson, artist, Lubbock, Texas, ink on 17" x 23" watercolor paper, "The Bell Home – 209 Grant".

Virginia Mahaley Thompson, artist, Lubbock, Texas, ink on 17" x 23" watercolor paper, "China Doll" Erwin Home.

Virginia Mahaley Thompson, artist, Lubbock, Texas, ink on 17" x 23" watercolor paper, "Ellis County Courthouse – Waxahachie, Texas".

Kelly Carlson-Reddig, architect/educator, "travel sketches", pen, ink and pencil, various sizes.

112

Kelly Carlson-Reddig, architect/educator, "travel sketches", pen, ink and pencil, various sizes.

James C. Watkins, MFA, artist/educator, "travel sketch", Shinto Shrine, Hikone Japan, ebony pencil on 10" x 12" drawing paper.

114

James C. Watkins, MFA, artist/educator, "travel sketch", Shinto Shrine, Hikone Japan, ebony pencil on 10" x 12" drawing paper.

115

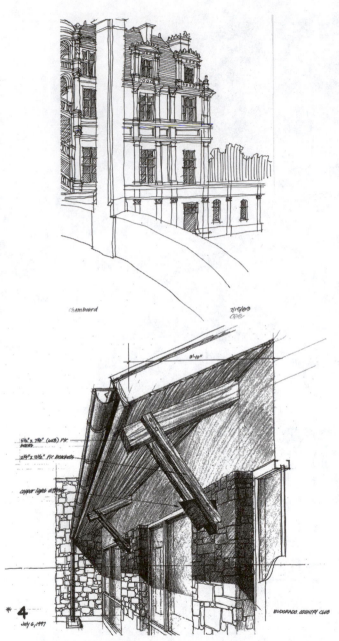

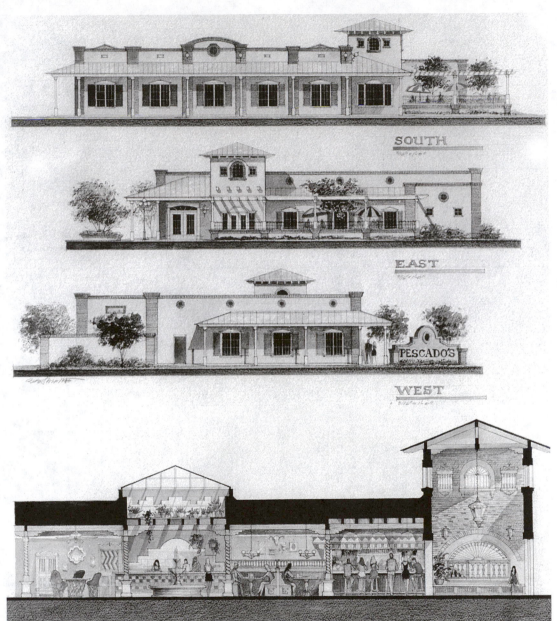

SOUTH

EAST

WEST

Carl Ede, architect, Three Architecture, Dallas, Texas, Ink and pencil on 11" x 17" drawing paper.

Ben Shacklette, architect/illustrator, elevations and section Scheme III Pescado's, Lubbock, Texas, watercolor and colored pencil.

116

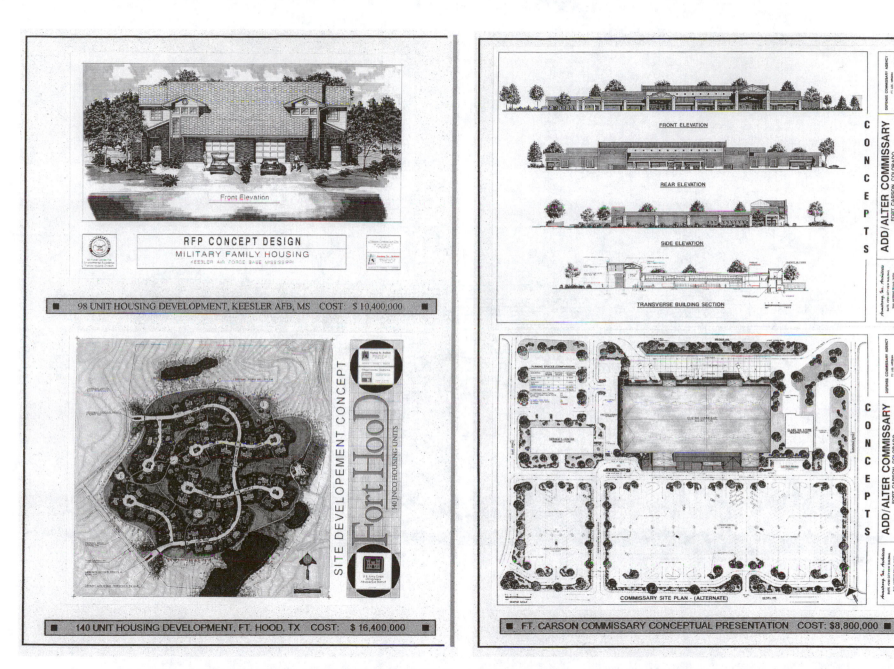

98 UNIT HOUSING DEVELOPMENT, KEESLER AFB, MS   COST: $ 10,400,000

140 UNIT HOUSING DEVELOPMENT, FT. HOOD, TX   COST: $ 16,400,000

FT. CARSON COMMISSARY CONCEPTUAL PRESENTATION   COST: $8,800,000

Ted Armstrong, architect, Armstrong Inc., Family Housing and Fort Carson Commissary, marker and pencil.

Lloyd Lumpkins, architect, Fusch - Serold & Partners, Dallas, Texas, Highland Park Residence, pencil and ink on 11" x 17" vellum.

Robbie Fusch, architect, Fusch - Serold & Partners, Dallas, Texas, Residence, pencil on 14" x 19" vellum.

Robbie Fusch, architect, Fusch - Serold & Partners, Dallas, Texas, Child's Playhouse, pencil on 11" x 17" medium weight white drawing paper.

Robbie Fusch, architect, Fusch - Serold & Partners, Dallas, Texas, Guesthouse Residence, pencil on 11" x 17" medium weight drawing paper.

Robbie Fusch, architect, Fusch - Serold & Partners, Dallas, Texas, Residence, pencil on 12" x 18" medium weight white drawing paper.

122

Robbie Fusch, architect, Fusch - Serold & Partners, Dallas, Texas, Inglenook Study, Residence, pencil on 12" x 18" medium weight white drawing paper.

123

Evelyn Davis, designer, Davis and Associates, Lubbock, Texas, watercolor and marker on board.

Phil Hamilton, illustrator, Looney Ricks Kiss Architects, Memphis, Tennessee, Residence, ink on 11" x 17" drawing paper.

Phil Hamilton, illustrator, Looney Ricks Kiss Architects, Memphis, Tennessee, Sheraton Suites Hotel in Irving, Texas, ink on 11″ x 17″ drawing paper.

Phil Hamilton, illustrator, Looney Ricks Kiss Architects, Memphis, Tennessee, Island Park Condominiums, ink on 11″ x 17″ drawing paper.

Phil Hamilton, Illustrator, Looney Ricks Kiss Architects, Memphis Tennessee, Clock Tower Plaza University of Memphis, ink on 11" x 17" drawing paper.

Phil Hamilton, Illustrator, Looney Ricks Kiss Architects, Memphis, Tennessee, Project for a Country Home, ink on 11" x 17" drawing paper.

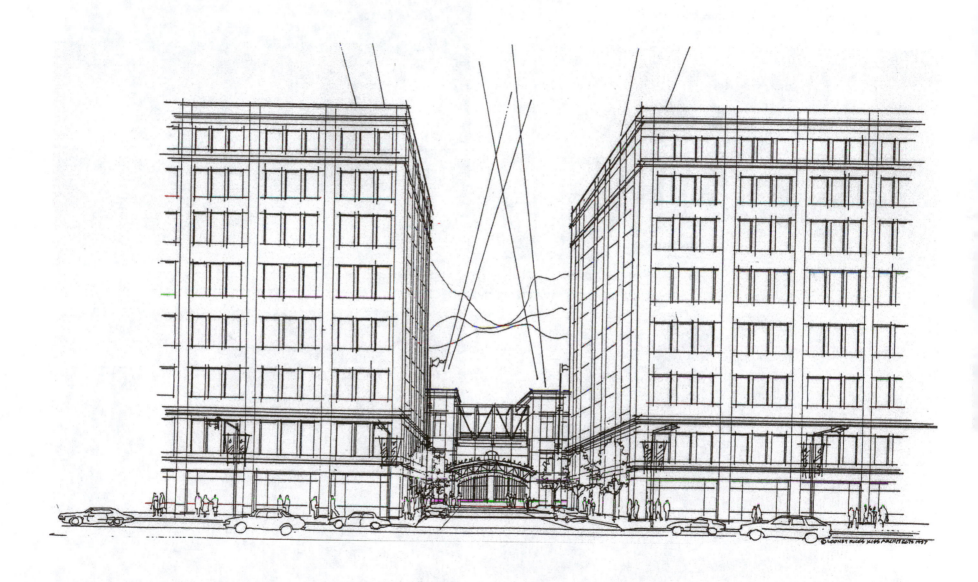

Victor Buchholz, illustrator, Looney Ricks Kiss Architects, Memphis, Tennessee, Study for Urban Renewal, ink on 11" x 17" drawing paper.

129

John Tran, architect, Leo A Daily, Dallas Texas, Public Tour Conceptual Competition @ Western Currency Facilities, Fort Worth, Texas, black marker on 11" x 17" drawing paper.

Tom Sherold, Ilustrator, Demaresat & Associates, Dallas, Texas, (LEFT) Mid Rise Apartments, (RIGHT) University of West Florida, both watercolor on 11" x 17" watercolor paper.

130

PERSPECTIVE VIEW @ TOUR BRIDGE

Nestor Infanzon, architect, Leo A Daly, Dallas, Texas, Public Tour Conceptual Competition @ Western Currency Facilities, Fort Worth, Texas, black marker on 11" x 17" drawing paper.

Nestor Infanzon, architect, Leo A Daly, Dallas, Texas, Lamar University – Orange Campus Library and Academic Building, ink and color pencil on 11" x 17 drafting paper

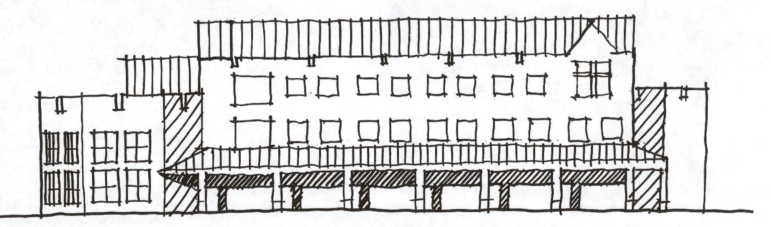

David Sacha, architect, Leo A Daly, Dallas, Texas, Lamar University – Orange Campus Library and Academic Building, ink on 11" x 17" drafting paper.

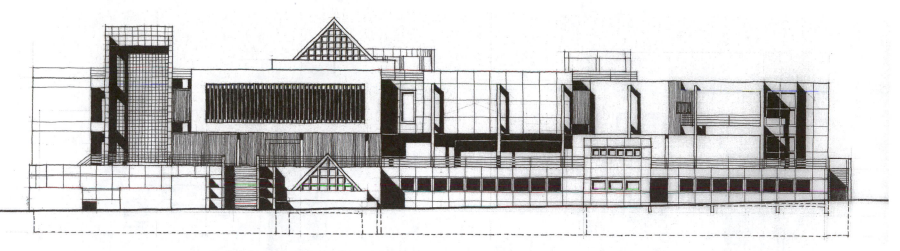

D. Nowak, architect, Nowak Group, Lubbock, Texas, Elevation Study, Ink on 11″ x 17″ tracing paper.

Michael Peters, architect, Michael Peters AIA, Lubbock, Texas, Private Office Building, ink on 12″ x 24″ vellum.

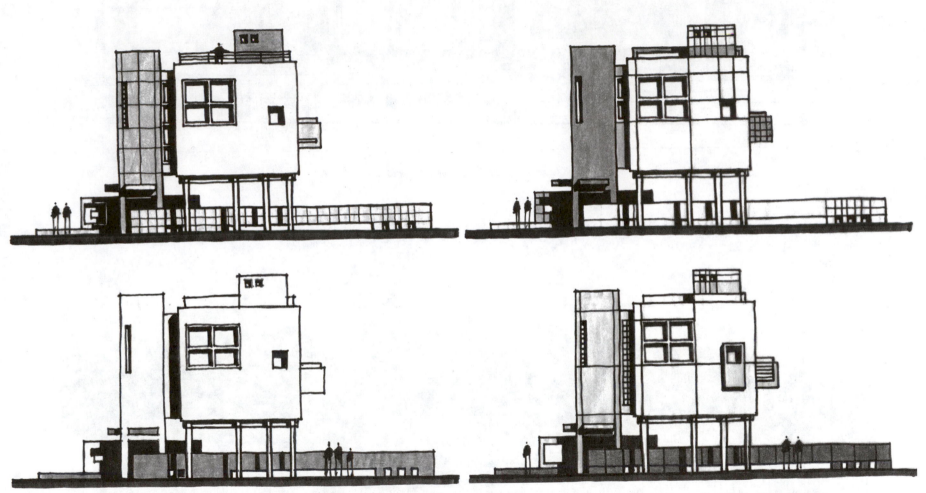

D. Nowak, architect, Nowak Group, Lubbock, Texas, Design Concept Study Drawings, (Lakeway, Texas House), felt-tip and color pencil on 10" x 12" trash paper.

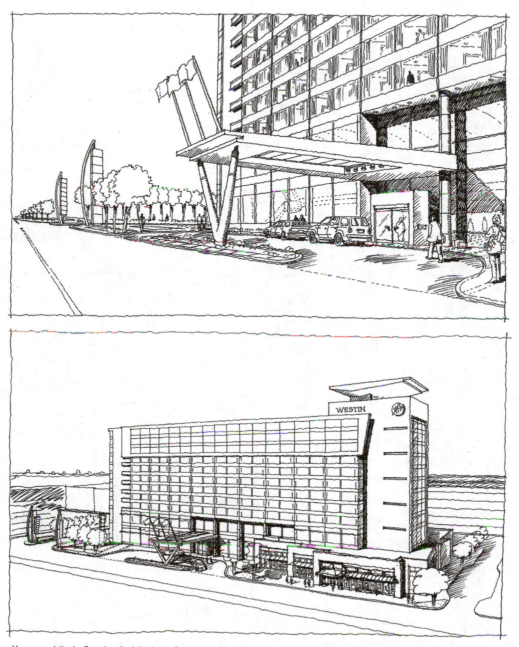

Lester Yuen, architect, Gensler Architecture, Design & Planning Worldwide, Houston, Texas, ink on 11" x 17" drawing paper.

Lily Sun, architect, Leo A Daly, Dallas, Texas, Degolyer Library Renovation, Southern Methodist University, ink on 11" x 17" drafting paper.

Gary Pitts, architect, PSA Architects, Dallas, Texas, Dallas Police Headquarters, color pencil and color marker on 48" x 36" butcher paper.

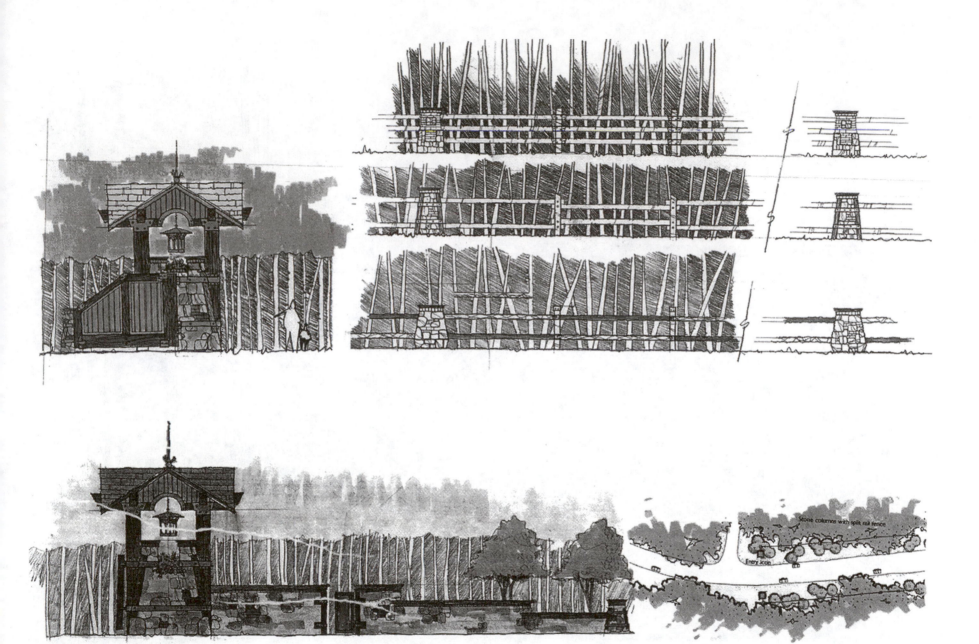

Mesa Design Group, landscape architects, Dallas, Texas, Windermere Schematic Design Concepts, ink and marker on 36″ x 42″ trash paper.

138

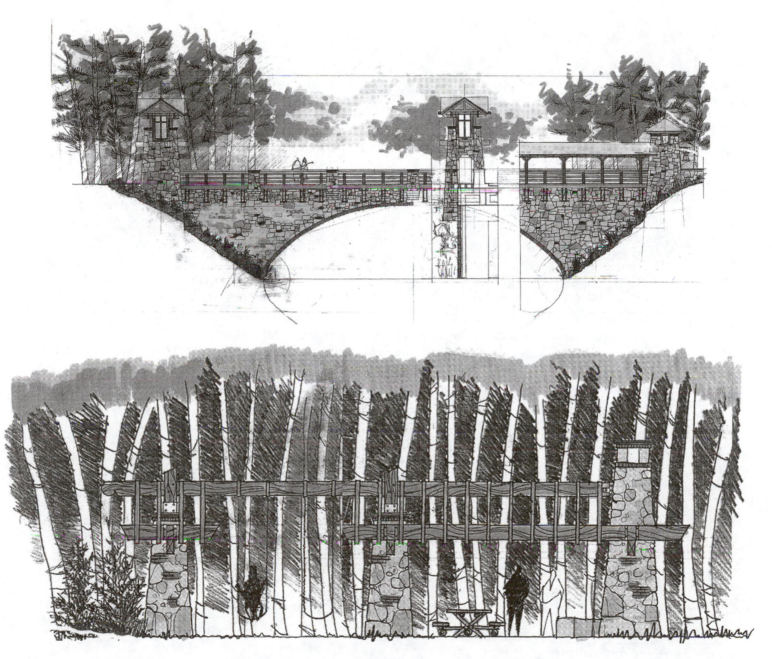

Mesa Design Group, landscape architects, Dallas, Texas, Windermere Schematic Design Concepts, ink and marker on 36" x 42" trash paper.

139

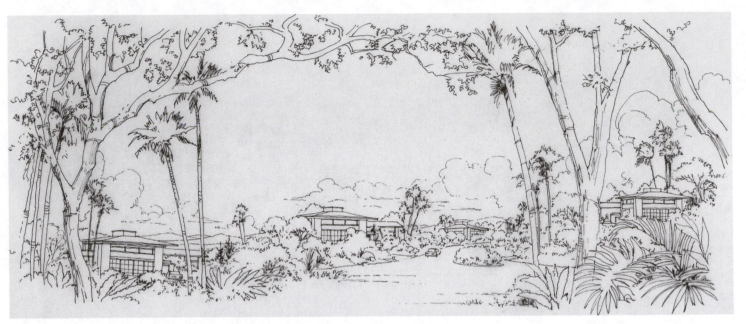

Lily Sun, architect, Leo A Daly, Dallas, Texas, Xi Li Lake Villas, Hong Kong, ink on 11" x 17" drawing paper.

Nestor Infanzon, architect, Leo A Daly, Dallas, Texas, Xi Li Lake Villas, Hong Kong, ink on 11" x 17" drawing paper.

140

David Farrell, architect, Good Fulton & Farrell Architects, Dallas, Texas, watercolor on 22" x 30" watercolor paper.

David Farrell, architect, Good Fulton & Farrell Architects, Dallas, Texas, watercolor.

David Farrell, architect, Good Fulton & Farrell Architects, Dallas, Texas, color pencil.

Interior View

(concept drawing)

David Farrell. Architect, Good. Fulten and Farrell Architects, watercolor and marker on prints.

144

Independent Study

Independent study offers unique opportunities to explore the universe of architectural illustration. Here are four examples of the variety of excellent products that may be achieved with the proper motivation. The first is a more conventional architectural rendering that is a tour de force in pen and ink by Stephen Doyle. The second is somewhat less conventional. It is exploration of humor in architecture presented in the form of a comic strip by Ryan Molloy. This project was proposed by the student and proved to be an excellent device for developing board layout design. The third project, also by Ryan, is an innovative merger of computer and freehand drawing. The fourth project by Sam Lin is an award winning work specifically done for "The Annual Ken Roberts Architectural Delineation Competition" in Dallas, Texas.

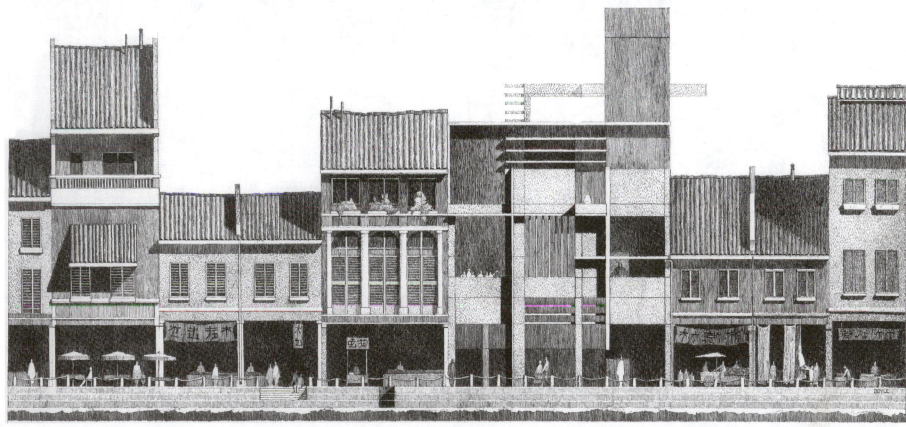

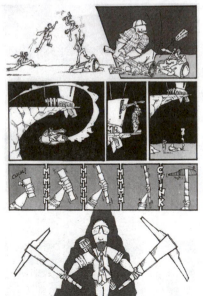

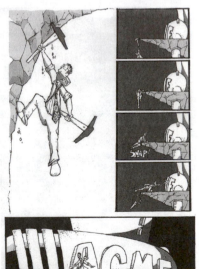

146

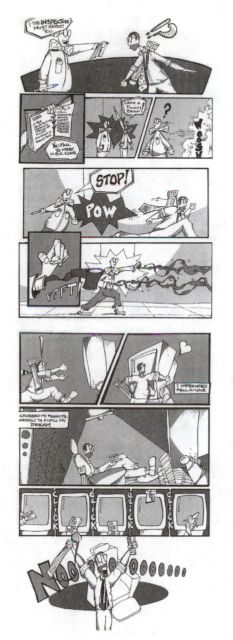

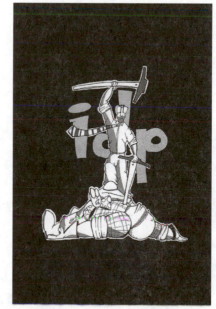

147

Auxiliary

Due to production constraints, we were unable to present all student projects used for this course in earlier sections of this publication. They are presented here in an abbreviated form along with some additional images of projects presented earlier. Many of these projects were done in full color, but are shown here in grayscale as supporting examples.

Student drawings by Sam Lin, Estaban Cantu, Michael Bryan and Kevin Witt.

Student Bird House Competition winner by Paula Yeager, watercolor on watercolor block, 15" x 20". Winners of this competition receive cash awards and build the birdhouses to be sold at a charity auction. Second semester, color class final presentations by Michael Zimmerman and Eric Pate, watercolor and mixed media on 3 11" x 17" boards. Drawing from a model by Alfonzo Zavala., color pencil on yellow tracing paper.

Student drawings, interior color studies, color pencil on yellow trace by Reggie Savage and Michael Bryan. Elevation study by David Farrell, architect, Good Fulton Farrell Architects, Dallas, Texas, watercolor on board. Isometric drawing demonstrations by J. Davis various papers and media, 8 1/2" x 11".

151

Student painting done as a special problem in an advanced delineation class, this mixed media collage/painting by Alfred Bryce was originally intended as a competition entry. The original painting is on cardboard and measures approximately 5 1/2' x 3'.

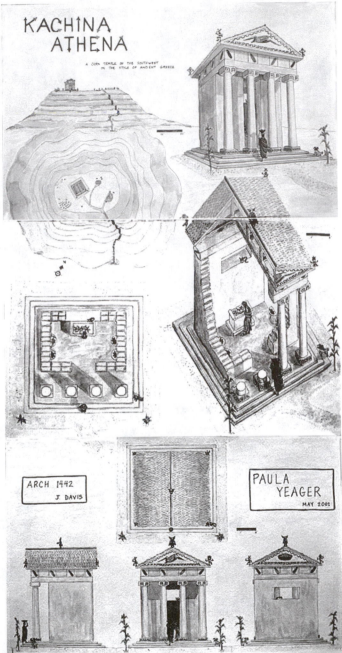

Student illustration, second semester, color class final project by Paula Yeager, watercolor on bristol board, 3 - 11" x 17" boards.

152

Student drawing by Clint Garwood, watercolor on 15" x 20" watercolor paper.

Student drawing by Seth Parker, watercolor and color pencil on 15" x 20" watercolor paper.

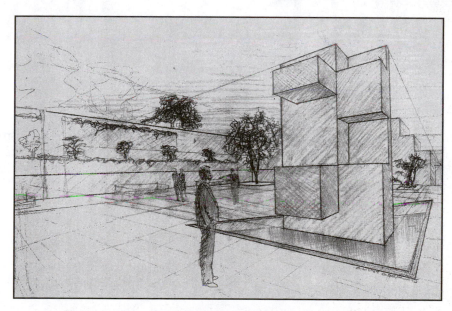

Student drawing by Clint Garwood, color pencil on 15" x 20" tracing paper.

153

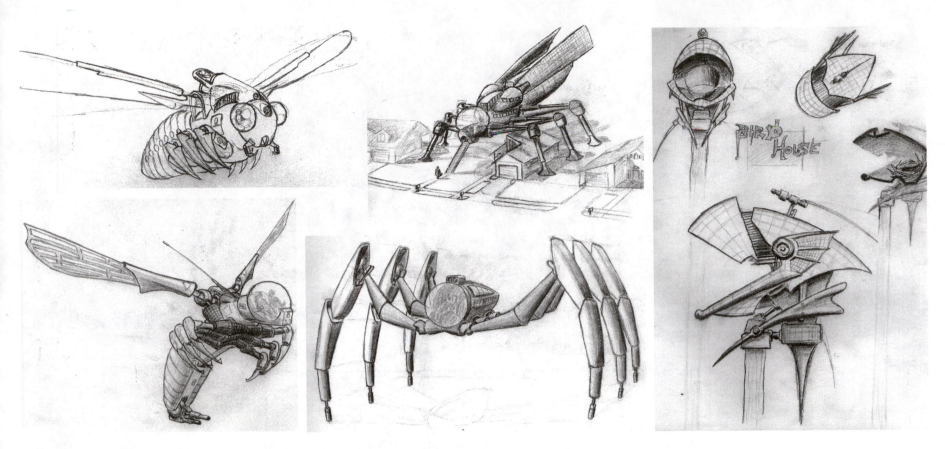

Sketch Diary

Each student is expected to maintain a daily sketch diary which will document their thoughts, dreams, fantasies, plans, aspirations and visual problem solving. The rules are simple. Make an entry every day. It may include sketchs, poetry, or even cut-outs of magazine images you wish to remember and document, collaged in with class notes and drawings you made while waiting for a bus. The sketch book drawings on this page evolved into a fantastic entry for a bird house competition design. The drawing and notes on the next page are typical example pages from an upper level architecture students sketch diary.

Goals
Develop the habit of recording your thoughts and draw every day.

Methodology
Keep a permanent sketch diary and learn to enjoy it.

Pages from a sketch diary by Sam Collins.

Daily sketch diary pages from student sketch book by Jim Gunn, various media, 8.5" x 11".

155

Student drawings, top, color pencil by Brian West and Seth Parker, bottom, watercolor and color pencil on 14" x 24" cold press illustration board.

156

Axonometric Shade and Shadow Work Sheets

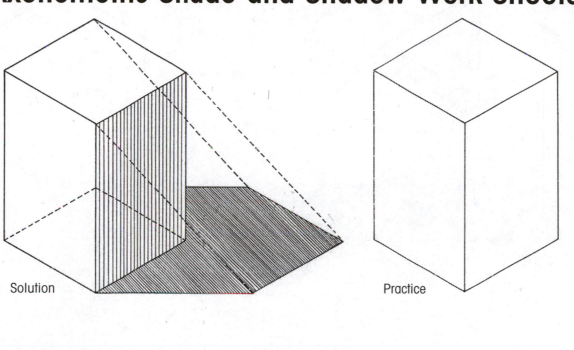

Solution

Practice

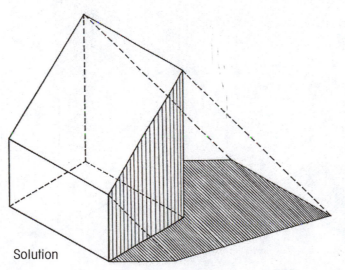

Solution

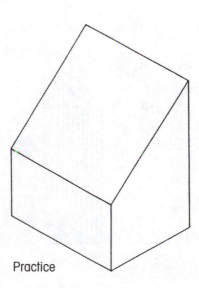

Practice

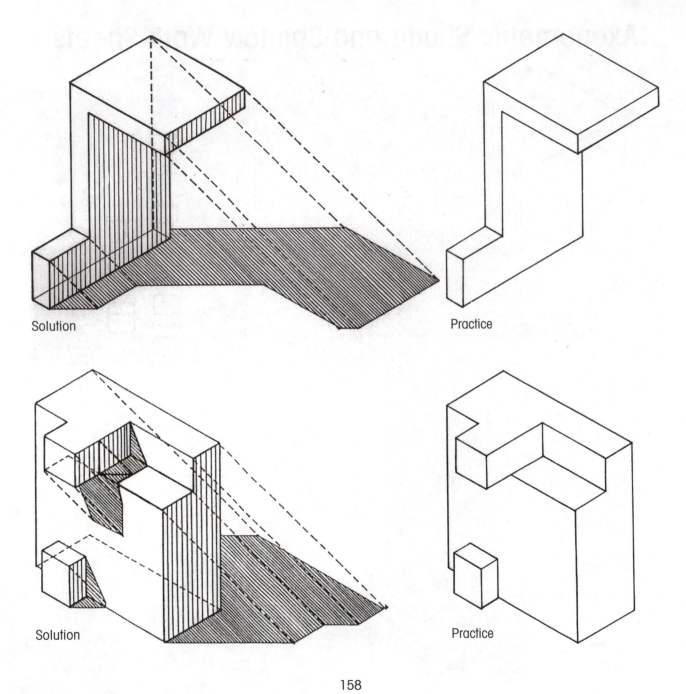

Solution

Practice

Solution

Practice

158

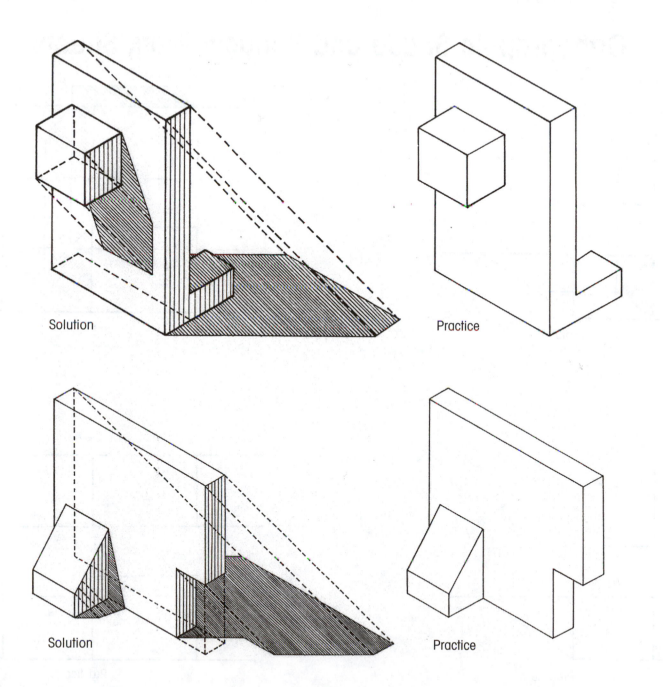

Solution

Practice

Solution

Practice

159

Orthographic Shade and Shadow Work Sheets

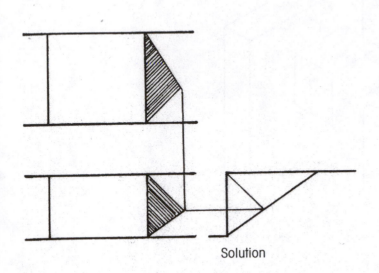

Solution

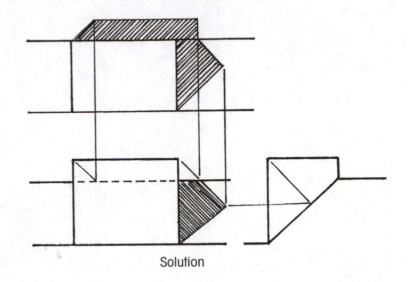

Solution

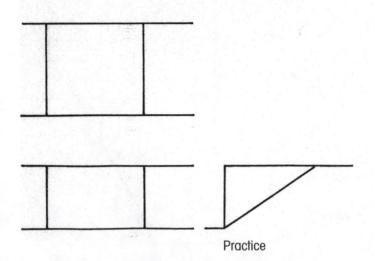

Practice

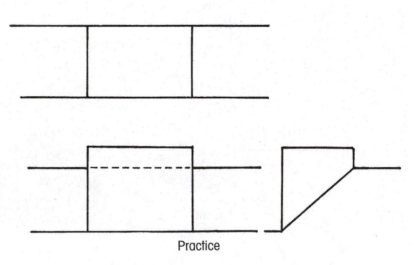

Practice

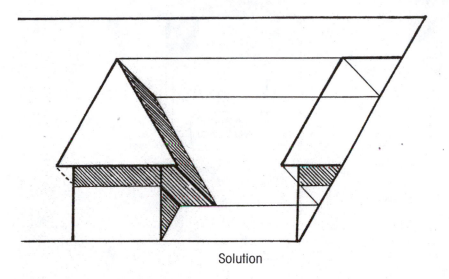

Solution

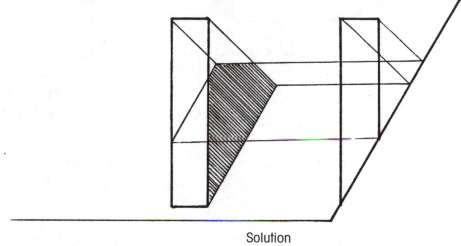

Solution

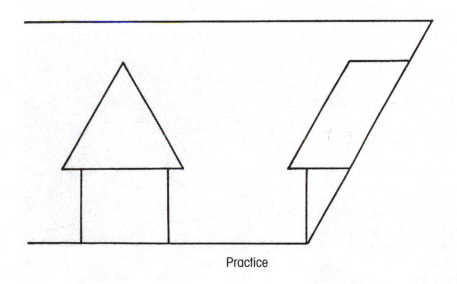

Practice

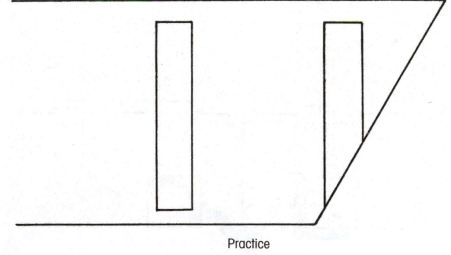

Practice

161

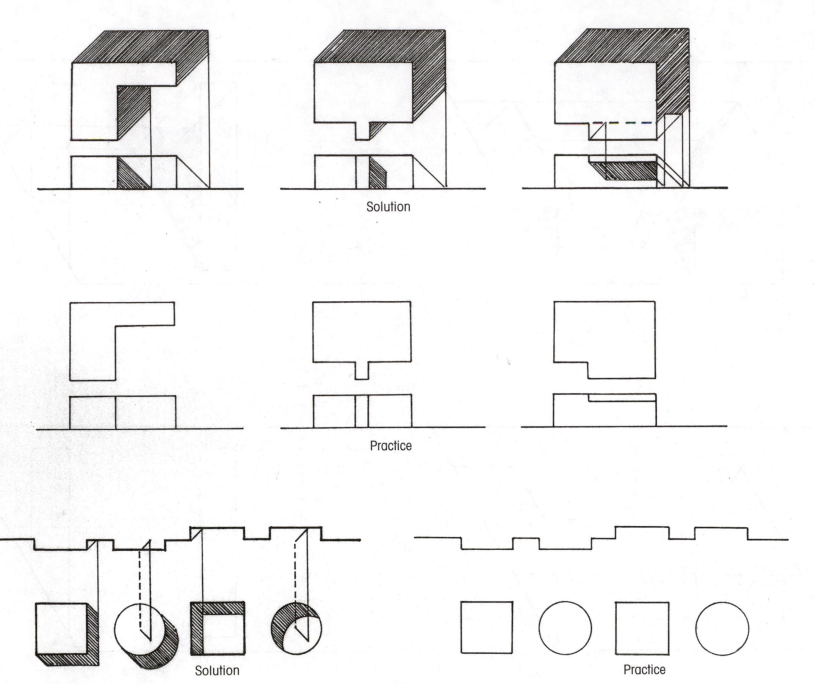

Solution

Practice

Solution

Practice

162

Glossary

Aerial Perspective- visual phenomenon where forms appear less distinct as they recede in space because of the greater density of the air between the viewer and the object.

Analogous- three related colors. Hues allied to each other due to their side by side relationship on the color wheel.

Analogous with Complement- three colors allied to each other by their adjacent relationship on the color wheel with the addition of the hue diametrically opposite the central hue of the three.

Axonometric Drawing- a paraline drawing of an axonometric projection with all lines parallel to the three principal axes drawn to scale (includes isometrics), any diagonal or curved lines are distorted. Any pictorial graphic that shows three faces of an object in one orthographic view may be classified as an axonometric.

Cast Shadows- the shadows projected upon a surface by an object that stands between the surface and the light source.

Color Harmony- the organization of colors that create a *pleasant stimulation*. There are two methods, which may be used, either separately or in combination to produce harmony in hue. One method is through the use of complementing colors. The other is by means of closely associated hues.

Composition- the organization of elements in a pictorial space.

Complementary- colors that are diametrically opposite each other on the color wheel. When these colors are place side by side, each makes the other appear more intense. When they are mixed in equal proportion they neutralize one another.

Construction Drawings- sometimes called working drawings. These are accurate graphic or pictorial indications of the design, location, dimensions and relationship of the elements of an architectural project.

Construction Lines- lines used to organize and simplify complex forms by reducing them to basic geometric shapes.

Contour Line- a line that follows the edge of the form, or travels across the surface, without shading or modeling the form.

Convention- the use of a common visual language, application of standard rules of drawing for a specific purpose. In drawing architectural plans certain types of lines always mean the same thing, such as short dashed lines used to represent object lines that are hidden from view.

Design Drawing- any drawing made to aid the visualization, exploration and evaluation of a concept; a drawing made during the design process.

Divider- a mechanical drawing instrument used for dividing space into equal units and it is handy for making quick, accurate, repeated measures.

Drafting- drawing with the aid of instruments, usually to scale indicating dimensional specifications; also called mechanical drawing.

Elements- the components that make up a drawing, or design - line, shape, form, space, value, texture and color.

Entourage- contextual elements such as people, cars, furniture, plants and landscape features; images of one's environment or surroundings used to compliment architectural delineation.

Eye Level- in perspective drawing the eye level is the same level as the horizon line.

Fenestration- an architectural opening, the design of a door or window.

Form- the shape of an object indicating mass. The shapes used in abstract design.

Gesture Drawing- quick scribbles or marks designed to show movement or action by flowing over and through the interior of a form or composition. Visual shorthand, often used as a foundation for more extended drawing or to establish structure. Gesture drawing is usually developed from the whole to the part.

Highlight- a line or area of very bright light on the surface of a form directly illuminated by the immediate light source.

Horizon Line- the line where the earth and sky meet.

Hue- the identification of a color by name, i.e., yellow, blue, red, etc.

Intensity- the saturation level of a hue. A *fully saturated* hue can be described as being *more intense* than duller colors of the same hue dimension.

Intermediate Colors- colors that fall between a primary color and a secondary color; also called *tertiary colors*.

Linear Perspective- a perspective system in which forms get smaller as they recede in space, receding parallel lines converge at a vanishing point. Also called "vanishing point perspective."

Line Quality- the appropriate use of line type and weight for good visual communication. Sharp clear lines advance. Light, thin, and broken lines recede. Varied or modulated line weight adds vitality to a freehand sketch, a heavy, even line profiles a paraline drawing and defines space.

Monochromatic- the use of one color. In this color scheme the color may vary in value and chroma from light to dark.

Monochromatic With Complement- the variation of one color from light to dark or from dark to light used with its complementary color.

Negative Space- the space around an object or the shape of the space between objects.

Orthographic Drawing- a type of pictorial graphic in which all lines of sight are perpendicular to the picture plane. This type of drawing is appropriate for showing measured dimensions.

Paraline Drawing- any single view drawing characterized by parallel lines remaining parallel to one another.

Perspective- any of several methods for representing three-dimensional objects on a two-dimensional surface as they appear to the eye.

Picture Plane- the imaginary transparent plane that represents the drawing surface on which the image of a three- dimensional object is projected.

Poché- solid areas of a built form that are cut in a floor plan or section drawing, usually indicated in black or by hatched lines.

Presentation Drawing- a single rendering or set of drawings done to communicate a design proposal for exhibition, review or publication.

Primary Colors- red, yellow and blue on the Prang color wheel (some other systems of color organization use different nomenclature). Colors which can't be made by mixing other hues.

Reflected Light- the light that appears on the edge of a shadowed form because of the reflection of light off an adjoining plane.

Rendering- a drawing of a building or interior space artistically delineating materials, shades and shadows. Usually it is a perspective drawing or painting done for presentation.

Section- a view of an object as it would appear when cut through by an intersecting plane. Sections are drawn to show the interior of a form and are usually done as an orthographic projection to scale.

Secondary Colors- colors that fall between two primary colors.

Shadow Core- the darkest portion of the shaded area on a rounded form.

Split Complementary- a split complementary is made up of three colors, one hue and the two colors on either side of the opposite complementary hue.

Space- the distance between two points or the area or volume between specified boundaries, negative area between objects.

Spatial Profile- emphasis on object lines depicting the edges where solid form meets spatial void; typically, the heaviest line weight in a paraline drawing.

Spatial Indicators- the use of line and tone in a drawing to give the impression of three-dimensionality and depth.

Station Point- the position of the observer in relation to the object in view.

Tetrad- any four colors that are equidistant on a color wheel and whose connecting path forms a square inside a color wheel.

Tonal Drawing- a drawing built primarily of areas of gray as opposed to a line drawing.

Tonality- when using multiple color schemes, tonality refers to the dominance of a single color that would be common in each color scheme.

Tone of Line- creating the illusion of gray or graduated value with black and white. Crosshatching with pen and ink drawing is an example of use of tone of line.

Triad- any three colors that are equidistant on a color wheel and whose connecting path forms an approximate equilateral triangle inside a color wheel.

Trompe l'oeil- a drawing or painting rendered to emphasize the illusion of reality, usually with extreme detail.

Value- the range of dark and light. Value also refers to the location of a color's relationship to white and black. A light color such as a yellow is *high* on the value scale (closer to white) and a dark color such as a violet or blue is *low* on the value scale (closer to black).

Vignette- a drawing that gradually fades into the surrounding paper leaving no definite line at the border.

Index

Portfolio Contributors

Ted Armstrong, architect, Woolpert LLP, Dallas, Texas, 117
Victor Buchholz, illustrator, Looney Ricks Kiss Architects, Memphis, Tennessee, 129
Carl Ede, architect, Three Architecture, Dallas, Texas, 108, 116
James T. Davis, artist – educator, Texas Tech University, Lubbock, Texas, 99
Evelyn Davis, designer, Davis & Associates, Lubbock, Texas, 124
David Farrell, architect, Good Fulton & Farrell Architects, Dallas, Texas, (cover), 98, 100, 141, 142, 143, 144, 151
Richard Ferrier, architect, Associate Dean UT Arlington School of Architecture, Arlington, Texas, 73, 96, 97, 105, 106, 107, 108
Robbie Fusch, architect, Fusch – Serold & Partners, Dallas, Texas, 100, 119, 120, 121, 122, 123, 24
Phil Hamilton, illustrator, Looney Ricks Kiss Architects, Memphis, Tennessee, 103, 124, 125, 126, 127, 128
Nestor Infanzon, architect, Leo A Daly, Dallas, Texas, 131, 132, 140
Christopher J. Kupcunas, architect, Principal. Bryant, Burton, Kupcunas Architects Dallas, Texas, 109
Lloyd Lumpkins, architect, Fusch – Serold & Partners, Dallas, Texas, 118
Mesa Design Group, landscape architects, Dallas, Texas, 138, 139
Danny Nowak, architect, Good Fulton & Farrell Architects, Dallas, Texas, 133, 134
Paul Stevenson Oles, architect, Interface Architects, Newton, Massachusetts, 95, 105
Michael Peters, architect, Michael Peters AIA, Lubbock, Texas, 133
Gary Pitts, architect, PSA Architects, Dallas, Texas, 137
Kelly Carson-Redding, associate professor, University of North Carolina at Charlotte, Charlotte, North Carolina, 112, 113
David Sacha, architect, Leo A Daly, Dallas, Texas, 132
Ben Shacklette, architect – educator, Texas Tech University, Lubbock, Texas, 101, 102, 116
Tom Sherold, illustrator, Demarest & Associates, Dallas, Texas, 130
Lily Sun, architect, Leo A Daly, Dallas, Texas, 136, 140
Virginia Mahaley Thompson, artist – educator, Texas Tech University, Associate Professor Emeritus, Lubbock, Texas, 110, 111
John Tran, architect, Leo A Daly, Dallas, Texas, 130
James C. Watkins, artist – educator, Texas tech University, Lubbock, Texas 114, 115
Bin Yu, architect, Demarest & Associates, Dallas, Texas, 104
Lester Yuen, architect, Gensler Architecture, Design & Planning Worldwide, Houston, Texas, 135

Additional Credits

Cover design by James C. Watkins and James T. Davis
Illustration on dedication page by James T. Davis
Authors' photograph by John Q. Thompson

References and Bibliography

Architectural Drawing, Yee, Rendow, John Wiley & Sons, Inc., N.Y., 1997

Architectural Presentation Techniques, Atkin, William Wilson, Van Nostrand Reinhold Co., N.Y., 1983

Architectural Drawing, Porter, Tom, Van Nostrand Reinhold, N.Y., 1990

Architectural Illustration in Watercolor, Hoffpauir, Stephan and Rosner, Joyce, Whitney Library of Design, N.Y., 1989

Architectural Rendering Techniques/A Color Reference, Lin, Mike W., John Wiley & Sons, Inc., N.Y. 1985

Architecture In Pen And Ink, Chen, John, McGraw-Hill, Inc., N.Y., 1995

Design Basics, Lauer, Davis A., Holt, Rinehart and Winston, N.Y., 1979

A Visual Dictionary of Architecture, Ching, Francis D. K., Van Nostrand Reinhold, N.Y., 1997

Design Drawing Techniques, Porter, Tom and Goodman, Sue, Charles Scribner's Sons, N.Y., 1991

Drawing and Painting Architecture, Evans, Ray, Van Nostrand Reinhold Company, N.Y., 1983

Drawing on the Right Side of the Brain, Edwards, Betty, J.P. Tarcher, Inc., Los Angeles, 1979

Drawing The Creative Process, Simmons, Seymour and Winer, Marc, Prentice-Hall, Inc., Englewood Cliffs, New Jersey, 1977

Design Drawing, Ching, Francis D.K., Van Nostrand Reinhold, N.Y., 1998

Entourage: A Tracing File for Architecture and Interior Design Drawing, Burden, Ernest, McGraw-Hill, N.Y., 1981

Graphics for Architecture, Forseth, Kevin, Van Nostrand Reinhold Company, N.Y., 1980

The Airbrush In Architectural Illustration, Karsai, Tibor K., Van Nostrand Reinhold, N.Y., 1989

The Art of Architectural Drawing, Schaller, Thomas Wells, Van Nostrand Reinhold, N.Y., 1997

The Complete Illustration Guide for Architects, Designers, Artists and Students, Evans, Larry, Van Nostrand Reinhold, N.Y., 1993

The Natural Way To Draw, Kimon Nicolaides, Houghton Mifflin Company, Boston, MA., 1969

Tiny Houses, Walker, Les, Overlook Press, Woodstock, N.Y., 1987

Tracing File for Interior and Architectural Rendering, McGarry, Richard M., Van Nostrand Reinhold, N.Y., 1988

Understanding Architecture Through Drawing, Edwards, Brian, E & FN Spon, London, UK, 1994

Post Script

To students of architecture, other books which we recommend on architectural drawing and architects in love with art follow.

An Architect in Italy. Mauduit, Caroline Clarkson N. Potter, Inc./Publishers, N.Y., 1988
An Architect's Paris. Carlson-Reddig, Thomas and Kelly.* Bulfinch Press Book, Little, Brown and Company, Boston, 1993.
Andrea Palladio: the Four Books of Architecture. Placzek, Adolf, Dover Publications Inc., New York, 1965.
Architectural Drawing: The Art and the Process. Allen, Gerald and Oliver, Richard. Whitney Library of Design, New York, 1981.
Architectural Illustration. Oles, Steve.** Van Nostrand Reinhold Co., New York, 1979.
Architectural Visions: the Drawings of Hugh Ferriss. Leich, Jean Ferriss, Whitney Library of Design, New York, 1980.
Architecture in Watercolor. Schaller, Thomas W. Van Nostran Reihold, N. Y., 1990.
Color in Architectural Illustration. Rochon, Richard and Linton, Harold. Van Nostrand Reinhold, N. Y., 1989.
Carlo Scarpa. Los, Sergio and Frahm, Klaus. Benedikt Taschen, Hamburg, 1993.
Drawing the Future. Oles, Paul Stevenson.** Van Nostrand Reinhold, N. Y., 1988.
Eric Mendelsohn. Whittick, Arnold. F. W. Dodge Corp., New York. second printing, 1956.
Masterpieces of Architectural Drawing. Powell, Helen and Leatherbarrow, David. Abbeville Press. New York, 1982.
New Techniques of Architectural Rendering, Second Edition. Jacoby, Helmut. Van Nostrand Reinhold, N. Y., 1981.
Piranesi, Early Architectural Fantasies. Robison, Andrew. The University of Chicago Press. Chicago, Il., 1986.
Rob Krier on Architecture. Krier, Rob. St. Martin's Press, N. Y., 1977.
Taking Tea with Mackintosh. Kinchin, Perilla. Pomegranate Communications, Inc., Box 6009, Rohnert Park, CA 94927, 1998.
The Great Perspectivists. Stamp, Gasvin. Rizzoli, N.Y., 1982.
The Venetian Hours of Henry James, Whistler and Sargent. Honour, Hugh and Fleming, John. A Bulfinch Press Book, Little, Brown and Company, Boston, 1991.
200 Years of American Architectural Drawing. Gebhard, David and Nevins, Deborah. Whitney Library of Design, New York, 1977.

These are books which I like to have near and hold in my hand again and again.
Virginia Mahaley Thompson, Associate Professor Emeritus, College of Architecture, Texas Tech University. B. Advertising Art and Design, Department of Architecture and Allied Arts Texas Tech, 1959.

*   Kelly Carlson-Reddig is a Texas Tech graduate with a B. Arch., 1986.
**   Paul Stevenson Oles, Jr., FAIA is a Texas Tech graduate with a B. Arch., 1960.